MATISSE

His Life and Complete Works

SOPHIE MONNERET

In Collaboration With
SIMON AND HÉLÈNE MONNERET

LONGMEADOW
P R E S S

For this present English
language edition:
Todtri Productions Limited,
New York

ISBN: 0-681-10475-9

Printed in Spain by
Fournier Artes Gráficas, S.A.

Editor:

Clotilde de Bellegarde

Designer:

Luis F. Balaguer

Editorial Assistants:

José Antonio Vázquez

Patricia Núñez Millieri

Rosa Vallribera i Fius

Albert Pujol Gámiz

English Translation:

Richard Jacques / Discobole

Design Assistants:

Manuel Domingo Pérez

Miguel Ortíz Català

Publishing Assistant:

Monserrat Juan Peña

Contents

H.matisse

Henri Matisse was born in Cateau-Cambrésis, in the north of France on 31 December 1869, the eve of the year which saw the fall of the Second Empire and the proclamation of the Republic.

His parents, who both came from that small town, lived in Paris for some years after their marriage. Émile Matisse, his father, worked in a textile store; Héloïse, his mother, was a dressmaker in Passy. When they returned later to their native Picardy, to Bohain-en-Vermondois in the Aisne, the Matisses abandoned textiles and opened a grocer's shop, which was soon successfully turned into a store selling grain and paints. Héloïse Matisse prepared the colors herself and Émile carefully chose the finest grain at the corn market in Paris.

That atmosphere, a blend of the rationalism of his father – a hard-headed businessman – and the artistic sensibility of his mother, certainly exercised an influence on the young Henri Matisse. In 1914 he wrote to Charles Camoin, his fellow student at Gustave Moreau's studio: "I am a romantic, but with a good scientific, rationalist half, which is the root of the struggle from which I sometimes emerge victorious, but out of breath."

Brought up in the heart of the textile country, Henri Matisse showed a decided taste for fabrics at a very early age and devoted great attention to choosing his clothes. This taste can be seen in the works of the last years of his life, when he created tapestries and costumes for the theatre and painted drapes or vestments and chasubles for the Dominican chapel in Vence.

He went to primary and secondary school in Bohain and at the Lycée Henri-Martin in Saint-Quentin, receiving a classical education in which Latin and Greek occupied a prominent place. In 1887 his father sent him to Paris to study for his law examinations and to find a "serious" profession. Those legal and classical studies endowed him with a penchant for reasoning and argument which remained with him all his life. During his time in the capital, the young Henri Matisse never visited a museum or showed any interest in painting or art of any kind.

Two years later, with a qualification in law, he went to work as clerk to a solicitor in Saint-Quentin.

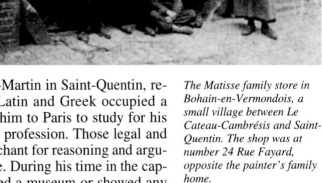

The Matisse family store in Bohain-en-Vermondois, a small village between Le Cateau-Cambrésis and Saint-Quentin. The shop was at number 24 Rue Fayard, opposite the painter's family home.

APPRENTICESHIP

Matisse awoke late to art, unlike Picasso who from the age of seven, drew animals to order, starting with the legs or the tail as requested.

It was in 1890, on the occasion of a long convalescence after an operation for appendicitis, that he took an interest in painting; the man in the next bed passed the time by copying colored reproductions. He asked his mother for a box of paints, and thus he took his first steps in the art of color. He had found his vocation. He had barely recovered before he enrolled at the municipal design school, the Quentin de La Tour Foundation, where he spent an hour every morning before going to work. The foundation trained students in the decorative arts, mainly the decoration of fabrics. Sometimes they were given a portrait by La Tour to copy, loaned by the Musée Lécuyer, which had conserved some of the master's pastels. Matisse discovered the fundamental duality between the observation of nature as it really is in its material form, and the painter's inner need to escape from that and bring to life on the canvas not the object to be painted, but the emotion, the feelings which bind him to that object.

Every free moment he had he took up his brushes and painted frantically through the evening until nightfall. His Sundays were given over to visits to the museums in the cities of the North, Lille in particular, which had a rich collection of Flemish painting.

His first canvas, *Still Life with Books* (1890), displays a realist application which evokes the Flemish still lifes of the 17th century. Though rather clumsy, the painting was undoubtedly at the root of his decision to return to Paris to learn to paint. For Matisse wanted to go to Paris, where a group of daring artists, the "Impressionists," having shattered the established order of official painting and provoked public and critics alike, were now enjoying recognition.

Émile Matisse was somewhat hostile to his son's vocation. "You'll starve to death," he told him. But Héloïse supported him and even managed to persuade her husband to give Henri a remittance of 100 francs a month to help him live in the capital.

Matisse, in the center, poses in 1892 with his fellow-students at the Académie Julian. The master's style of teaching was not at all to his taste because of the "perfection" of the figures that were the order of the day.

Armed with a letter of introduction from a painter friend in his region, Paul-Louis Couturier, addressed to William Bouguereau – a famous academic painter who directed a studio at the Académie Julian – Henri Matisse left for Paris early in 1891. He immediately enrolled at the Academy, but his stay there was a short one, as he was annoyed by Bouguereau's inflexibility and his conventional style of teaching. The young man began to attend the École des Arts Décoratifs, where he met Albert Marquet, who soon became his closest and most loyal friend. After a few failures in "competitions for places" he was officially admitted in 1895, with his friend, to the École des Beaux-Arts, to Gustave Moreau's workshop which both of them had attended regularly as observers since 1893. On the advice of the master, they went to the Louvre to copy David, Raphael, Poussin, Ruysdael, Boucher, Delacroix and, most of all, Chardin, from whom Matisse acquired his taste for soft light and interiors. During those years he worked hard, did a variety of exercises, and with Albert Marquet, painted landscapes in the open air and delicately classical still lifes, such as *The Blue Decanter* (1895). Gustave Moreau had a considerable influence on his art. The man that Henri Matisse called "the admirable master" awoke him to the problems of values, contrasts, intensities, harmonies, and the alchemy of colors. He was an incomparable teacher and the respect of this Symbolist for the personalities of his students gave free rein to their development. After Gustave Moreau's death in 1898, Matisse, Georges Rouault, Charles Camoin, Manguin, Jules Flandrin, and Henri Evenepoël were among the members of a small group of friends bound by a special intimacy which came from the memory of the painter.

By 1895 he had settled at number 19 Quai Saint-Michel, in a building which had been home to generations of painters. One of his neighbors was Émile Wéry, who practiced a discreet Impressionism. In the summer Matisse accompanied him on a first visit to Brittany and returned with some rather lackluster landscapes and seascapes with the same tone as the still lifes, in which gentle harmonies continued to prevail over color.

Gustave Moreau, Jason *(Louvre Museum, Paris). According to Matisse, Moreau told his students: "Do not just go to the museum; go down into the street."*

In 1896, he showed four paintings at the Salon de la Société Nationale des Beaux-Arts, among them a *Woman Reading* bought by the government for the Château de Rambouillet and a studio interior. He was proposed by Pierre Puvis de Chavannes and elected associate member of the Salon "for the quality of his work," which allowed him to send five canvases the following year: three still lifes and two interiors, among them *The Dinner Table*.

THE LURE OF COLOR

In Belle-Île, during the summer of 1896, Henri Matisse met John Russell, an Australian painter and disciple of Monet, who introduced him to Impressionism and gave him two drawings by Vincent Van Gogh, whom he had known well. Under his influence, Matisse began to lighten his tones and bring to his palette a few bright colors which he dabbed on the canvas with brief strokes. But the real revelation of Impressionism for him was his visit to the Caillebotte Collection in the Musée du Luxembourg, where paintings by Claude Monet, Edgar Degas, Auguste Renoir, Camille Pissarro, and Alfred Sisley were finally on show in 1897, after endless, sometimes dramatic, wrangling between the government and the Caillebotte family. In two of his paintings dating from 1898, *The Door of the Old Mill* and *The Courtyard of the Old Mill*, the Impressionist touch is evident and Matisse's personality begins to emerge. The same year, on the advice of Pissarro, he travelled to London and discovered Turner. For him, as for the Impressionists around 1870, it was a genuine revelation. Turner ignores the material presence of forms and concentrates on the forces, the energy which moves the universe, the visualization of atmosphere. With Turner, light transcends reality.

Shortly after his marriage to Amélie Parayre, a girl from Toulouse, in 1898 Henri Matisse travelled to Corsica. He was dazzled by the Mediterranean light: "It was in Ajaccio that I was first astounded by the South," he wrote later. The canvases he painted then, whether on "the island of beauty" or in Toulouse just afterwards, are there as proof: *My Room in Ajaccio, The Patient, The Olive Trees, Corsican Landscape.* In the last painting, the use of an Impressionist handling frees the artist from a minute description of objects. The pure tones which foreshadow his later stylistic choices are already present. At the same time, Matisse discovered the Japanese crepes so dear to the "Nabis," the group of post-Impressionist artists whose style was profoundly marked by Japanese art.

After a period in Toulouse during which their first son, Jean, was born, the Matisses returned to Saint-Michel in Paris. Henri went back to the École des Beaux-Arts, where Fernand Cormon, the master of prehistoric scenes, had replaced Gustave Moreau. Hostile to the unacademic painting of his pupil, Cormon forced him to leave the studio.

With his friend Marquet, Matisse painted in the Luxembourg Gardens, in the streets, and as Cézanne and Guillaumin had done before him, in the suburb of Arcueil, constantly enriching his palette with ultramarines, emerald greens, and oranges. The volumes are also increasingly simplified (*Rue à Arcueil*).

THE BLACK YEARS

In 1899 Matisse gave up any hope of an official career, which deprived him of a whole range of middle-class customers. With no fixed resources, he was obliged to accept "bread and butter" jobs. He designed the laurel friezes which decorated the Grand Palais for the Universal Exhibition in 1900. Amélie opened a clothes shop. Although short of money, Matisse bought from Vollard a plaster by Auguste Rodin (the bust of *Henri Rochefort*), a drawing by Van Gogh, a Gauguin (*Young Man with the Flower of Tiaré*), and *The Three Bathers* by Paul Cézanne, a painter who was to exercise a major influence on him. To pay for all those works he sold his wife's engagement ring. Nevertheless, he still attended studios with Marquet, notably the Académie Camillo, Rue du Vieux-Colombier, where Eugène Carrière, a painter of "hazy" family scenes, taught. There he met some of the members of what was to be the "Fauves" group, among them André Derain, who in turn introduced him to his friend Maurice de Vlaminck in 1901, at the time of the

Vincent Van Gogh retrospective, so crucial to the advent of Fauvism. Matisse was thirty-one when his second son, Pierre, was born. He was an imposing man, tall, with a bushy beard, whom Vlaminck described in these words: "Blue eyes behind gold-rimmed spectacles, red beard, Henri Matisse looked serious and had a vague air of 'Herr Professor' about him." Nevertheless, his health was delicate; in 1901, he had to spend a time in the Alps to recover from a severe attack of bronchitis. There he rather half-heartedly painted a few landscapes: "I don't think mountain landscapes can be of use to painters. The difference of scale is an obstacle to any kind of intimate contact," he wrote later to Raymond Escholier. Back in Paris, Quai Saint-Michel, the artist tirelessly painted the view of the banks of the Seine, Notre-Dame, and the Île-de-la-Cité. *Notre-Dame with Violet Walls* is one of the most beautiful paintings from that period of poverty. In 1901 he took part for the first time in the Salon des Indépendants, of which Signac was the life and soul. With his friends he exhibited at Berthe Weill's gallery; in

Matisse, his wife Amélie and his daughter Marguerite at the house in Collioure in 1907, after he had painted Luxe I, *which can be seen behind the artist. Matisse wrote, "As soon as I arrived in Collioure, I began to paint nature forgetting about any method or, rather, without becoming a slave to one."*

April 1902 she sold one of his paintings for 130 francs. But sales were few and far between and his health was still frail. In 1902 his wife, exhausted by the worries of a flagging business, finally persuaded him to return to Bohain where the cost of living was cheaper. That was a tragic period and Matisse even thought of abandoning painting and finding a job behind a desk. However, he painted a few canvases, among them *Studio under the Eaves,* and began to sculpt, an art for which he had followed several courses in 1899 at the École Étienne Marcel. Two of his statuettes were exhibited at the Salon d'Automne in 1904.

The summer of 1904 spent in Saint-Tropez with Paul Signac, where they were joined by Henri-Edmond Cross, prompted Matisse to adopt the manner of the two painters: neo-Impressionism. The technique, perfected by Georges Seurat after the optical theories of Chevreul, Helmholtz, and Rood, uses the colors of the spectrum in small dots juxtaposed according to the principles of Divisionism. Signac's exhibition in 1904 at the Galerie Druet and a reading of his book *D'Eugène Delacroix au néo-impressionnisme* (1899) delighted him. His most representative canvas of the time, *Luxe, calme et volupté*, was hung at the Salon des Indépendants in 1905 and bought by Signac.

Eugène Druet was a former café owner and photographer whom Rodin saw regularly. He had become an art dealer and in 1903 he moved to the Faubourg Saint-Honoré; his gallery was a rallying point for the painters of Matisse's generation. It was a time of friendly gatherings: Gertrude Stein and her brothers Leo and Michael (wealthy American art lovers who had settled in Paris), Henri Manguin and others, all had their open day. The talk was about painting, friends took tea together. At Gertrude and Leo Stein's, Matisse met Pablo Picasso; they were to have a lifelong friendship tinged with rivalry. At Michael and Sarah Stein's he got to know and like Matthew Prichard, who introduced him to Georges Duthuit, later to become the husband of Marguerite, his eldest daughter. Vollard exhibited paintings of his in 1904 and bought some from him at a low price. Hostile by nature to any kind of technical constraint and ill-at-ease with a procedure which did not allow him to express all his inner emotions, the painter cut short his neo-Impressionist experience. He did not abandon the method completely, but adapted it to his own temperament,

Edward Sleichen took this photograph of Matisse (1909) in his studio at Issy-les-Moulineaux, when he was sculpting La Serpentine. *Critics called Matisse's sculptures: "...insufferable parodies of the human form."*

producing an entirely different pictorial expression which marked a turning point in his life and work: *The Bathers, Blue Nude (souvenir of Biskra), Luxe I, La Pastorale*. The last canvas shows a new independence of stroke and color which foreshadows Fauvism.

FAUVISM

The revolution took place in 1905, during the summer spent in Collioure with Derain. Daniel de Montfreid, whom they visited in Corneilla-de-Conflent, showed a fascinated Matisse the canvases which Paul Gauguin had sent him from Tahiti and introduced him to the sculptor Maillol, who became a good friend. Those influences led Matisse to a new way of painting. The colors are carried to paroxysm; the transitions worked with lighter shades harmonize the violent hues with one another, the touch is prolonged and the burst of light is intensified. Matisse painted *The Roofs of Collioure*, *Open Window in Collioure*, then *Woman in a Hat*, which was the centerpiece of the Salon d'Automne and was purchased by the Steins. At that Salon, not only the works of Matisse but also those of Derain, Vlaminck, Manguin, Camoin, Puy, and Rouault staggered the public with their expressive violence. At the center of the gallery where they were hung, a statuette depicting Donatello looked so incongruous that Louis Vauxcelles entitled his article in the magazine *Gil Blas* "Donatello in the wild beasts' cage". A word was born, Fauvism – "fauve" means wild beast in French – and a style which the Germanic countries practiced with even greater violence under the name of Expressionism. Soon disparaged by an extremely intellectual movement, Cubism, French Fauvism was to be short-lived. It nonetheless marked a break by endowing color with the independence which was to be one of the constituent elements of abstract art.

Although Matisse rejected the label "Fauve," his ascendancy over his colleagues made him the leader of that style, to which Van Dongen and Matisse himself remained faithful until after 1910. The period left him with a taste for the primary, root colors; in his own words, "for a major impact on the feelings of the person looking at them."

Matisse would never disown the influences he had been subject to, whether of the academic painters or the Impressionists. "I owe my art to all painters," he said in 1949. Paradoxically, he rejected the weight of the past, fiercely criticizing the teaching of the École des Beaux-Arts, and glorified adventure, audacity, the abandonment of conventional painting. That duality recurs in practically all his works; it is what makes them so rich. In fact, one of the main features of his art is his independence from fashions and currents, which meant that he could borrow one technique,

Life, *bronze sculpture from 1906 (private collection), signed by Henri Matisse.*

then another, and immediately return to a more classical handling by combining new ways of displaying the colors or setting the line.

Because of this, Matisse eludes all classification, all schools. From his first canvas to his last creation, he was engaged in a tireless search for inner balance, perfect unity between man and the world.

THE FIRST FRUITS OF SUCCESS

Matisse's career really took wing from 1906-1907. He was thirty-seven and had the means to travel. North Africa attracted him in 1906: Algiers, Constantine, Biskra. There he discovered African art, ceramics, and craft weaving. A true journey of initiation whose memories and impressions were the origin of his painting *Blue Nude*. He painted some large scale compositions, such as *La Joie de vivre*, a representation of the myth of Eden which was bought by Leo Stein after the Salon des Indépendants in 1906.

An exhibition organized in the same year by Druet scored a notable success and collectors became increasingly interested: the Steins, Marcel Sembat, the socialist MP for Montmartre, Gustave Fayet, and Shchukin, a wealthy Russian merchant who already owned paintings by Cézanne, Renoir, and Gauguin, acquired some of his canvases in 1907. The artist had just made a tour of Italy (Padua, Florence, Arezzo, Siena), also crucial to the evolution of his painting, which would then take account of the syntheticism of Giotto and the monumental style of Piero della Francesca. Irrefutable proof that he had become a master, Matisse opened a teaching studio in 1907 at the instigation of Sarah Stein and the German painter Hans Purrmann. The young man, who had come to Paris to see the Manet retrospective at the Salon d'Automne of 1905, discovered Matisse there and became his most fervent disciple.

The studio was installed in 1908 in the former convent of the Sacré-Cœur (today Musée Rodin). The neighbors regarded the various tenants of the building with suspicion. Rodin, who pinned indecent sketches to his walls, a Rumanian comedian of doubtful morals, and a singer at a café-concert rubbed shoulders with a "Fauve" called Matisse in that merry band which was later joined by Jean Cocteau.

The lessons he gave his pupils, mostly Scandinavian or German, helped to spread Fauvism and trained some excellent painters, among them the Norwegian Per Krogh and the Swede Nils Dardel. The Académie Matisse was to function for two years with about sixty students. "From Monday to Saturday," its creator confided, "I tried to take those sheep and make them into lions. That made me expend a great deal of energy. Then I thought: should I be a teacher or a painter? And I closed the studio."

His first exhibitions abroad (New York, Moscow, Berlin) were held in 1908, the year in which he visited Germany with Purrmann. During the stay, as he said himself, he "had a wonderful time and got very tired... the best thing we did was some steady drinking of cold Munich beer and Rhine wine." An exhibition at the Cassirer Gallery brought him back to Berlin a few months later. Things turned out very badly; Cassirer refused to hang the canvases which Matisse had sent for fear of shocking his customers. So the 1909 exhibition never took place. Shortly before, in December 1908, Matisse had published an explanation of his research in the *Grande Revue* ("A painter's notes"). He put it into practice on two enormous canvases commissioned in 1909 by Shchukin for his town house in Moscow. All decoration is eliminated, he said, in order to attain "that state of condensation of sensations which makes the picture." Those two panels, *Dance* and *Music*, with systematically reduced colors, were hung in 1910 at the Salon d'Automne before being sent to Russia.

1909 was also the year when Matisse signed his first contract with Bernheim, who devoted a large exhibition (66 canvases) to him. That made it possible for him to acquire a property at Issy-les-Moulineaux and to have a studio built in the garden.

Kuwele mask (Musée des Arts Africains et Océaniens, Paris). Matisse was one of the first painters to take an interest in primitive art. He introduced Picasso to it.

THE ORIENTAL INFLUENCE

His journeys in Algeria and Morocco, his visit with Marquet to the exhibition "Masterpieces of Muslim Art," which brought all of Europe flocking to Munich in 1910, and his discovery of Spain mark the beginning of Matisse's interest in oriental art. In October 1911, when he was invited by Shchukin to Moscow to see how his works had been hung, he was astonished to discover the Byzantine style and the icons in Russian churches.

His first period in Tangier, late 1911 to early 1912, and his notes and impressions brought about a remarkable renewal of his visual repertoire. Nevertheless, when he disembarked, it was pouring rain: "Shall we see the sun in Morocco? What's to become of us? For two pins we'd go back to Paris to find the sun." Fortunately the rain stopped and Matisse painted one of his most beautiful canvases. Dazzled by the quality of the light and the nobility of the people of Morocco, as Delacroix had been before him, through the experience of the oriental world he discovered a sense of the sacred. In samples of that art he found models of purity, harmony and refinement which led him to say later, "The journeys to Morocco helped me to make the necessary transition and allowed me to rediscover a closer contact with nature which had never been possible from the application of a living, but somewhat limited theory, as Fauvism had been." Twenty or so canvases, notably the portraits of Zorah and Amido, *The Moroccan Café, Tangier, Landscape Seen from a Window, On the Terrace,* and *The Gate to the Casbah* illustrate those days in 1912-1913 shared with Marquet, Camoin, and the Canadian painter James Wilson Morrice.

The years after 1910 were also years of experiments with ceramics. And they were the time of the portraits in which his wife and children occupy a place of honor. *The Painter's Family*, painted in 1911, his most radically "Persian" canvas, features Amélie, Marguerite, Pierre, and Jean. Among them, Marguerite always remained his favorite model. They all lent themselves submissively to the artist's demands. They posed for hours in the studio; they sat in silence at table so as not to disturb his concentration; they followed him on exhausting walks intended to calm his nervous tension. Amélie encouraged him to refuse commitments and to innovate. Matisse's friends – painters, writers, musicians – also posed for him.

In 1912, he exhibited his sculptures for the first time in New York and took part in the post-Impressionist exhibition in London. A year later, the Moroccan paintings from his last journey to Tangier were presented at the Galérie Bernheim-Jeune. But most of all he was particularly well represented at the triumphant Armory Show in New York, where modern European painting conquered the United States.

Matisse photographed during his visit to Tangier in 1912.

THE WAR YEARS

When war broke out in 1914, the Matisses were in Issy-les-Moulineaux. Shortly after the Battle of the Marne the painter left for Toulouse, where Marguerite was staying, then went with Marquet to Collioure, where he made the acquaintance of Juan Gris, who was moving from analytical Cubism to synthetic Cubism at the time. After that meeting and another in Paris in 1915, Matisse embarked on a whole cycle of new investigations which reflected his attraction for Cubist dislocations. The result was a few experimental works: *Mademoiselle Yvonne Landsberg*, *White and Pink Head* (a portrait of Marguerite Matisse), *Bathers by a River*. But he was too attached to classical means of expression to persevere with that new path.

Matisse hardly stirred from Collioure, except to go to Menton to cure a fresh attack of bronchitis. On the way he stopped in Nice which, from 1916, became his haven, alternating with the apartment on the Quai Saint-Michel and the house in Issy-les-Moulineaux.

Music – he played the violin himself – occupied an important part in his life and was of great help to him at difficult times. There are echoes of it in his work in his violins and violinists, but most of all in the musicality of his figures, spun out like the notes of a melody.

That period marked one of the peaks of his career. Matisse was extraordinarily fertile: the *Lorette* series – she began to pose for

At the prompting of the ceramicist André Methey, Matisse decorated a number of objects, such as this vase (Musée de l'Orangerie, Paris), again inspired by the theme of dance.

him in 1915, still lifes (*The Colocynths*) or "where dark become light," studio interiors (*The Studio on the Quai Saint-Michel...*), new spatial investigations (*The Moroccans*). He also created dozens of lithographs and about seventy-five etchings or dry-points. With no news of his family – his sons Jean and Pierre were at the front – he lived in anguish and worked without a break to drive himself into a stupor. On the eve of war he had had an exhibition at Gurlitt's gallery in Berlin. During the black years, his works were on show in New York in 1915 and in London in 1916.

In 1917 he became close to Bonnard and visited Renoir for the first time in Cagnes. He had already stayed with him several times in Essoyes. He made his style as close to his as possible to evoke Renoir's *Garden*.

When Matisse was finally able to return to Bohain in 1918, he found the place in ruins; the family home had been bombarded. His mother died shortly afterwards.

During the break caused by the war, the collectors' milieu had been transformed. The Steins had hurried back to the United States, the Sembats were dead, Shchukin was in exile. His collections, with those of Morosov, formed the Museum of Western Art in Moscow in 1923. Other amateurs, often Scandinavian or American, took up the baton. The artist, who was turning increasingly towards investigations into form, uniting space, and musicality (*The Piano Lesson*), reassured the new collectors, less taken with the avant-garde than their predecessors. In 1918 he exhibited with Picasso at the Galérie Paul Guillaume. The preface to the catalogue was written by their friend Apollinaire, who died shortly afterwards.

THE RETURN TO REALISM

In the years following the war, Matisse adopted a new style which praised the sweetness of life. Certain features of Impressionism resur-

From 14 to 19 April 1913, the Bernheim-Jeune Gallery in Paris organized the "Henri Matisse exhibition of paintings of Morocco and sculpture". Marcel Sembat, a friend of the painter, remarked, "Do you remember that large canvas of a Moorish café? I recommend it. The whole of Matisse is concentrated in it." The canvas Sembat was talking about is The Arab Café, *hanging at the back of the room.*

faced in 1921, when he spent the summer in Étretat on the track of Monet. But most of all he painted the numerous portraits of women in interiors (*Interior in Nice: the Siesta*) and embarked on the long series of *Odalisques*; he painted dozens in different poses and costumes.

Matisse loved women and saw in each one the essence of "Woman." Their faces, which are often expressionless and even sometimes effaced (*Nude in a White Turban*), are of little importance. The line is all that matters. "Faced with a model, a woman or a flower," said Louis Aragon, "Henri Matisse's drawing has the enormous chastity of intelligence." Up to 1935-1940, he changed his female models frequently and behaved, as one of them said, in a "paternalistic and very possessive manner."

That first post-war period coincided for Matisse with fame: the Légion d'Honneur, the Carnegie Prize (1927), retrospectives in Copenhagen (1924) and Paris (1931), and numerous exhibitions all over the world. His work entered a new stage; he drew and engraved assiduously. He also travelled widely. He returned to Padua to see Giotto's frescoes and went to the United States in 1930 to be a member of the jury for the Carnegie Prize which was awarded to Picasso that year. Matisse then fulfilled a dream of his youth with a stay in Tahiti like Gauguin. Although he found it "appalling to have a whole day that starts with a blazing sun which doesn't change until it sets," the island seduced him with its light. He loved New York for its museums, its streets, and its skyline.

In the United States Albert Barnes, one of the leading collectors of Cézanne, Renoir, and Seurat, commissioned him to paint a picture for the grand hall of his foundation in Merion. The theme of dance was chosen once again, but completely restyled from *Dance*, which he had

done for Shchukin in 1910. The subject was difficult to treat: a surface of 52 square meters, with backlighting, divided into three panels. Matisse made sketches and numerous studies and experiments with colors. For the first time he used the technique of colored paper cut up with scissors. That allowed him to pin up the pieces of color, to move them around at will and thus to have a perfect preview of the position of the oil paintings which would replace them. The work was finished in 1932. Then came a terrible disappointment; some of the measurements were wrong. Matisse refused to consider any partial arrangements and redid all the faulty panels. The second version of *Dance* was finally completed in May 1933. He was sixty-three at the time.

While he was engaged on the work, between 1930 and 1932 Matisse illustrated an edition of Mallarmé's poetry published by Albert Skira. His superb etchings evoke the atmosphere of immaculate snowy purity created by the poet. From the regular, fine, sometimes almost invisible, line there emerge fairy-like creatures, like the nymphs of *L'Après-midi d'un Faune*. For Matisse, "painter and writer must act together, without confusion, but side by side. The drawing must be a plastic equivalent of the poem." In 1934 he did the engravings for James Joyce's *Ulysses*.

In 1920 Diaghilev had asked Matisse to do the sets and costumes for a ballet, *The Nightingale*. Stravinsky had composed the music and the choreography was by Léonide Massine. Massine worked with him again on *Farandole*, commissioned by the Ballets Russes in Monte Carlo in 1937 and performed again later with huge success with the title *Red and Black* at the Palais de Chaillot in Paris in 1939, and then in the United States. His interest in all forms of decorative art was also expressed through tapestry (*Papeete*, 1935, for Madame Cuttoli, *Song*, 1938, for Nelson Rockefeller).

Dance *(first version, Musée d'Art Moderne de la Ville de Paris). When Matisse visited Barnes in Merion the artist enthusiastically accepted the collector's suggestion to decorate the upper part of his dining room.*

The painter was working at the Hôtel Lutétia in Paris when the Second World War broke out. The exodus swept him to Bordeaux. He was to go to Brazil in June; his visa still gave him permission to leave, but he preferred to return to Nice. "My life is between the walls of my studio", he wrote in a letter to his son Pierre, who was living in New York. Settled since 1938 in the Old Hôtel Régina in Cimiez, Matisse worked twice as hard to alleviate the anguish which followed defeat. In 1941 an exhibition of his charcoal sketches and drawings was held at the Galérie Louis Carré. A serious operation in 1941 in Lyon confined him to bed for long periods. A long bamboo pole with a crayon on the end allowed him to draw on large sheets of paper pinned to the wall. It was in his bed that he illustrated *Le Florilège des Amours* by Ronsard (1941) and *Pasiphaé* by Montherlant (1941), no doubt recalling Gustave Moreau's painting of the mother of the Minotaur. In 1942 he did the poems of Charles d'Orléans and, in 1944, *Les Fleurs du Mal* by Baudelaire. Among the different versions of *The Rumanian Blouse*, (1940-1941), the one entitled *The Dream* is the condensation of a linearity which had become his primary goal.

His creative thrust remained absolutely intact, as proved by the retrospective of his work at the Salon d'Automne in 1945. Before and after that date, canvases increasingly purged of superfluous elements contrast the curves of a rocaille armchair or a wrought-iron table with great slabs of pure color (*Seated Dancer*, *Armchair*, *Still Life with Magnolia*, *Tabac Royal* (1943), *Large Interior in Red*).

THE MASTER OF LIGHT

In 1943 Matisse rented a house in Vence, the villa called "Le Rêve." Everything was designed to provide favorable conditions for work (a desk for drawing in bed, a revolving bookshelf within easy reach). Rare birds fluttered around an aviary; green plants, African masks, or Persian ceramics, works by friends and his own gouache cutouts created an intensely poetic atmosphere which is summed up in the admirable *Inhabited Silence of Houses* (1947). The cutout technique became his favorite form of expression. He used sheets of white paper hand-painted with gouache in the tones of his customary palette. "Cutting up the living color reminds me of sculptors carving from stone," he remarked. One of his most beautiful and accomplished works is the series of collages done between 1945 and 1947 for the book *Jazz*, the comments for which he wrote himself with his brush. When it came out in 1947, it was exceptionally successful. All his memories are condensed in it, in particular his journey to Tahiti in 1930 – the colors of the Pacific, the fauna and flora of the

In this self-portrait done with pen and Chinese ink, Matisse drew himself looking in a mirror in the manner of a caricature. His sense of irony is patent in this phrase: "I hope that however old we live to be, we shall die young."

Spring, a lino cut from 1938. That year, Matisse did his first lino cuts and Montherlant's Pasiphaè *had its premiere; the painter did the illustrations for it in 1943. In addition to Montherlant's work, in the nineteen-forties Matisse illustrated poetic works by Mallarmé, Ronsard, Charles d'Orléans, and Marianna Alcoforado.*

island. The whole work is airy and radiates that dazzling light which had revealed itself to him on the flight from London to Paris in 1937: "I have always been aware of another space in which the objects of my dreams evolve. I was looking for something other than real space." And he had found that space. It was the space of pure colors stripped of shadows and purely decorative shapes from which all subjective dimensions are excluded. The series of the large *Blue Nudes* from 1952 carry that purity of expression to its apogee.

Some of the gouaches have a simpler composition (single motif, restrained dimension). Between 1950 and 1953 his output was immense. He was eighty-two and he felt "in a hurry like a traveller packing his last suitcases." 1952 was notable for *The Negress*, inspired by the famous dancer Joséphine Baker, *The Parakeet and the Mermaid*, then *The Swimming Pool*, which is the crowning glory of the series. For Matisse there was no break between his earlier canvases and his cutouts: "With more absoluteness, more abstraction, I have attained a form trimmed down to essentials, and from the object which I used to present in the complexity of its space, I have conserved the sign which is sufficient and necessary to bring it to life in its own shape and in the setting in which I have conceived it." Immobilized in a wheelchair, he cut paper tirelessly, bringing joyous forms to life with his scissors like a happy demigod. He was tempted by sculpture once again. His correspondence with Henri Laurens describes his investigations.

It was in that atmosphere of intensive work and magnificent disorder that early in 1948 Matisse undertook a great adventure: the Dominican Chapel of the Rosary in Vence. "A church!" exclaimed Picasso. "Why don't you do a market instead?" Although he had been fairly indifferent to religion until then, out of friendship for his nurse he undertook a project which he saw as a means of going beyond his art.

With Brother Rayssiguier, Matisse drafted building plans, discussed the shape of the stained glass windows, the design of the ceramics, the liturgical objects and ornaments, and the vestments of the priests. Settled once again early in 1949 in the Régina, where the rooms were large enough for him to draw life size, he began with the windows for the nave and the choir and studied Grünwald's retable for the *Crucifixion*. The series *The Tree of Life*, composed of ultramarine, emerald-green, and lemon-yellow panes of glass, evokes the joy of living and vitality. The panes, like the great panels in white glazed terracotta squares with black-line drawings representing *Virgin and Child, The Via Crucis,* and *St. Dominic*, were based on innumerable sketches and drafts. Like Michaelangelo in the Sistine Chapel, Matisse devoted four years to his wish to give the world – and doubtless even more to give himself – the peace and hope of a spiritual space. "It is in the creation of the chapel of Vence," he said, "that I have finally awoken to myself." For the artist the building represented the fruit of his whole life, his masterpiece in which he finally managed to eliminate the superfluous and keep only the essential. At the same time he exhibited gouache cutouts at the Pierre Matisse Gallery in New York and then at the Museum of Modern Art in Paris, while two retrospectives of his work were organized in Philadelphia and Lucerne.

The Vence chapel was finished in 1950, the year the XXV Venice Biennale awarded him its major prize. Two years later came the inauguration of the Henri Matisse Museum in Cateau-Cambrésis with its collection of works donated by the painter.

Icarus, *gouache cutout, model for the book* Jazz, *published in 1947 (Musée National d'Art Moderne, Paris). Matisse said that the paper cutout allowed him to draw in color. "For me it is a simplification... I draw directly on the color, which is more measured since there is no transposition."*

Installed in the house in Vence, in 1946 Matisse painted Yellow and Blue Interior, *hanging on the wall. In it we can see the rocaille armchair in front of the fireplace.*

But the enormous effort he had expended on the Chapel of the Rosary had exhausted him. Matisse died on 3 November 1954 of a heart attack while he was still at the height of his creative vitality.

He had written to Rouveyre in 1950: "I hope that however old we live to be, we shall die young."

The paintings hanging behind Matisse are part of the Windows *series, the artist's last easel canvases, as he devoted his last years to the large works and the paper cutouts of forms and colors which were in constant renovation.*

THE DINNER TABLE, 1897
Oil on canvas, 100 x 131 cm
Private Collection

THE DINNER TABLE

This picture is Matisse's past, present, and future, a transitional work which summarizes the classical and modern influences he has received and foreshadows the aesthetic choices of the work he is still to do.

The first influence is a realistic one from the Netherlands and from Chardin. In this intimate genre scene, a composition is formed using objects from the traditional repertoire of still life painting – everyday items with their contrasting materials and shapes, such as tall, glass decanters; squat, rounded fruit; and bowls. This influence can also be perceived in the structural stability of *The Dinner Table*, which led Gustave Moreau to comment, "Those decanters stand so foursquare on the table that I could hang my hat on the stopper."

Next is the Impressionist influence, from Pissarro and Caillebotte. From them he borrows the vibration of touch which translates the effects of light on the material it bathes from behind and the coloring of the shadows, particularly perceptible on the white cloth. It is also an Impressionist investigation which gives the approaching plane effect, produced by the retreating perspective of the table cut off in the foreground of the picture, and the tight framing at the level of the far corner of the table and the young woman's lace cap. This person, who has already appeared in *The Bretonne Maid* from 1896, recalls the attitude of Manet's waitress in *The Bar at the Folies-Bergère*, standing behind her bottles, her plates, and her bowl of fruit.

But *The Dinner Table* also heralds, albeit timidly, Matisse's investigations into a new use of color which were to take him far away from Impressionism. As witness the prominent place of the orange in the first bowl of fruit and, in the foreground, the glass stopper of the decanter, which contains, like a cluster of precious stones made of pure juxtaposed colors, the full nocturnal range of the Fauves.

And so we can understand why this picture, which was presented at the Salon de la Nationale in 1897, brought Matisse into the heart of the controversy between academic and avant-garde critics.

STUDIO UNDER THE EAVES, 1903
Oil on canvas, 55.2 x 46 cm
The Fitzwilliam Museum, Cambridge

STUDIO UNDER THE EAVES

After *The Dinner Table,* Matisse went through a difficult period financially. He withdrew to Bohain and returned to a more conventional style of painting. With the picture we see here, he went back to an art of shaded values, objects in sharp relief, and strongly marked shadows. The dark tones and the monastic bareness of the room recall certain works by Rembrandt. The accentuation of the depth of field and the perspective provided by the low ceiling, together with the confinement of the color within acceptable limits, are all present in this return to his early work.

There is classicism too in this genre scene where Matisse has placed, opposite the easel, the motif of a work in progress: *Bouquet on a Bamboo Table.* Nevertheless, in this Nordic twilight Matisse remembers the summers he has spent in Corsica, and perhaps Turner, of whom he said later, "Turner lived in a cellar; every morning he threw open the shutters and then what incandescence! What dazzle! What jewellery!" The window in *The Dinner Table* was still closed. It was not until 1900 that the theme of the open window reached its fullest expression with the series of views of Notre-Dame and the Île-de-la-Cité, which he painted from his apartment on the Quai Saint-Michel. At that time

he used the window as a building block, with its verticals and diagonals which echo the rectangular architecture of the Paris landscape. Here the function of the window is to mark the symbolic threshold between two antinomic universes: the universe of values and the universe of colors. The window does not play the part of an opening onto the far distance, as it did in the golden age of perspective in the Italian Quattrocento. On the contrary, it reduces the distance between the exterior and the interior, brings the landscape into the studio, and serves to master its violence, which shatters the calm with its desire for light and color. A piece of luminous color captured in frontal perspective, the landscape glimpsed through the window in *Studio under the Eaves* already foreshadows a Fauvist painting.

28

**LUXE, CALME
ET VOLUPTÉ,** 1904
Oil on canvas, 98.5 x 118.5 cm
*Musée d'Orsay (on loan from the
Musée national d'Art moderne),
Paris*

LUXE, CALME ET VOLUPTÉ

A neo-Impressionist color technique, an art of drawing which is already decorative, a subject which is half bourgeois, half mythological.

Matisse had just spent the summer with Signac in Saint-Tropez when he started work on this picture. From his host he took the Divisionist manner of separating colors with a dab which is no longer Seurat's dot, but a small rectangle of pure color. This broadened touch marks a first break with Realism; the color has the purity of a rainbow, detaches itself from what it represents and functions on its own account. The Realist pane of glass misted up by the Impressionists is becoming opaque, abstract.

Matisse did not paint his picture from life, but in his studio, using a classical technique which consists of transposing a sketch done beforehand with a crayon on cardboard. He used the technique as a support for a decorative aesthetic, taking several motifs from Puvis de Chavannes. Like him, Matisse kept only the trunk of the tree, and the boat approaching the shore

looks like the one in *Doux Pays*.

The subject of *Luxe, calme et volupté* originates in part in *Le Goûter*, which depicts a woman, probably Madame Matisse, and a child on the beach by the gulf of Saint-Tropez. However, if the bourgeois family scene recurs in the picnic on the left of the painting, the three nude bathers are imaginary, and their monumental, heroic appearance refers back not only to Puvis de Chavannes but also to Cézanne; Matisse had acquired a small painting of bathers by him early on. The legend which Matisse is transposing here with his reference to Baudelaire's poem *L'Invitation au Voyage* is the bliss of the golden age. That legend ushers in the sense of the sacred in Matisse's painting.

The critics reproached Matisse for not respecting the modelling of forms by means of the gradation of colors, for painting his seated bathers with one leg green and the other pink, and for maintaining the preeminence of the line around the figures, as well as around the teapot and the cups.

**INTERIOR AT COLLIOURE
(THE SIESTA),** 1905
Oil on canvas, 60 x 73 cm
Private Collection

INTERIOR AT COLLIOURE (THE SIESTA)

This canvas conserves the blue, green, and pink range of the neo-Impressionists and a treatment of light which is close to the Impressionists. But it also marks a twofold break. First, the use of pure tones is no longer linked with the fragmentation of color with the touch; they are spread broadly in a single shade, treating the volumes as surfaces to be colored, like slabs. Then, although the line maintains a certain perspective through the objects (bed, chairs), the color no longer respects the outlines; it escapes them. As in a child's painting, the colors are the same inside and outside; the sun is the yellow dab on the wood of the bed; and the colors are the same on the child and on the objects: the same red for Marguerite's dress and the carpet.

In Matisse's work, sleep has modern connotations. The siesta, in an anonymous room – here a family boarding house, later a room with a view in a hotel – whose inhabitants are not identifiable – a girl with her back turned, a face without features. He also invents an interior which is no longer either academic or bourgeois, but transcribes a time in suspension, an immobility of beings and things which we find again in the work of neo-Realists such as Edward Hopper. A universe where the frame of the window and the balcony are a protection against the outside; cocooning? Matisse wrote later: "What I dream of is an art of balance, of purity and serenity devoid of troubling or disturbing subject matter... a mental balm, something like a good armchair in which one rests from physical fatigue." The soft, almost volatile colors, so fine that the canvas can be seen through the picture in places, reinforce the atmosphere of peace and timelessness.

But this moment of repose pushed to its absolute is also a moment of strangeness. Marguerite on the balcony is also Alice Through the Looking Glass, for the window is no longer an opening to the outside; it is a picture decorating the room in a child's dream of going out to play while her mother is asleep.

WOMAN IN A HAT, 1905
Oil on canvas, 80.6 x 59.7 cm
Museum of Modern Art (E.S. Haas
Collection), San Francisco

WOMAN IN A HAT

For Matisse the summer and autumn of 1905 were a journey through an experimental color laboratory. He simultaneously deepened his knowledge of Pointillism, painted some canvases with a violence of brush strokes which was close to Van Gogh and others with an almost abstract Japanese style, built with color as Cézanne did with geometry, and invented a new art of the decorative image. It was from that crucible that Fauvism emerged.

Woman in a Hat was painted when Matisse returned from a summer in Collioure accompanied by Derain, who infected him with a certain anarchic spirit which was common to the friends who met at Vlaminck's house in Chatou and whose works, collected at the Salon d'Automne in 1905, opened the way to Fauvism.

At first sight *Woman in a Hat* seems to be a product of emotional gesturing, piling pure tones on pure tones to detonate reality. That destruction by color is the beginning of a long series of pictorial aggressions which mark the art of the 20th century. However, behind this criticism of the pompous, bourgeois portrait, behind this weird representation of the face of the demi-mondaine (the bright red of the lips, the sharp black line of the eyebrows), a genre at which Van Dongen excelled, we can discern a wish for a pictorial reorganization of composition.

If the colored masses represented by the hat and the dress bear witness to Matisse's knowledge of the *haute couture* of his day, they also show the persistence in his work of a Cézanne-like organization of volumes. The hat, a fantastic still life, is a prodigy of balance where the volumes are created by the juxtaposition of pure colors applied with broad brushstrokes.

But there is also a reorganization of the face through the hierarchy of the features, the green line of the bridge of the nose making an almost ritual division of the two sides of the face in different colors. Not the make-up of a transvestite, but a Japanese mask or an icon, accentuated later in the portrait of *Madame Matisse*, which heralds the face-images of the decorative painters.

BLUE NUDE (SOUVENIR OF BISKRA), 1907
Oil on canvas, 92.1 x 140.4 cm
The Museum of Art (The Cone Collection), Baltimore

BLUE NUDE
(SOUVENIR OF BISKRA)

Blue Nude is an ancient statue fallen from a Fauvist sky into a primitive, symbolic garden of delights. From his journey to Algeria in 1906, Matisse brought back neither artistic enrichment nor anecdotal subjects. He wrote, "As for the belly dance, I did not look for it in Algiers; I'd watched a quarter of an hour it by chance in Biskra. Those famous 'Ouled-naïls' dancers, what a joke! I saw a hundred times better at the Exhibition." *Blue Nude* was not painted until 1907 in Collioure. Matisse, borrowing from Oriental art, uses the arabesque of the curved line of the stylized palm trees in the background to stress the forms of the body. In turn, the feet echo the drawing of the flowers and leaves. Also, the blue and red touches on the breasts and the lips – two precious stones or meteorites which glow like those on Persian plates made of enamelled metal.
But the construction

of space by means of successive stretches of color, with a figure in close-up emerging from the frame and detaching itself from a backdrop, is borrowed from Gauguin. Matisse's model is a sculpture he was working on at the time: *Reclining Nude I*. Having carelessly broken it, he wanted to conserve at least a trace. The realistic treatment of the body, its distorted shapes, and its relief come from the sculpture.

With this painting Matisse creates a new pictorial character: the living sculpture, a kind of Golem, the archetype of the model we find again in his other works, reclining or standing, painted or not painted, female or male, and which resurfaces in the work of a Surrealist like De Chirico.

This double has a complex genealogy: the anatomy of an academic nude, the mythological ritual nature of Cézanne's bathers, the opulence and generosity of the sculptures of Maillol, a friend of Matisse. And lastly, the influence of primitive art and of Gauguin, who had said: "The Eve of my choice is almost an animal," and from whom Matisse borrowed this Garden of Eden made of fairy colors; the sentimental dreamlike quality of Odilon Redon; and the Oriental mystery of Gustave Moreau's grottoes.

RECLINING NUDE I, 1907
Bronze, 34 x 50 x 28.5 cm
*Musée national d'Art moderne,
Paris*

RECLINING NUDE I

Reclining Nude I is one of the figures imagined by Matisse which became familiar in his work, both painting and sculpture, a little like the actors in the Commedia dell'Arte. It appears for the first time in a cult painting from 1905, *La Joie de Vivre*, in the form of a young nymph, very "Art Nouveau", in a bucolic Renaissance love scene. From that female figure the sculpture retains a refined elegance in the gesture of the raised arm, the movement of the provocative, lascivious pose resting on one hand and the thrusting out of the hip that puts the body on display.

We find the figure again in *Blue Nude (Souvenir of Biskra)* and a dozen later canvases, among them *The Music Lesson*. Matisse created his sculptures in stages. He usually began with a realistic phase close to Maillol and then introduced asymmetries, both in the lines of the face (inverse movements of mouth and nose) and in the disproportion of certain parts of the body (strong limbs but slender waist; angular, thrusting movement of the elbow, but exaggeration of the roundness of the hip); then he carved the surface in facets which catch the light. Each stage is visible in the final model.

Matisse sculpted *Reclining Nude* at Collioure and spent a good deal of time with Maillol, who was on holiday in Banyuls. All his life he conserved his admiration and friendship for him, even if he said: "Maillol's sculpture and mine have nothing in common; we never talked about the subject because we did not understand one another. Maillol worked with the mass like the ancients, and I worked with the arabesque like the Renaissance. Maillol did not like risks and I was attracted by them."

Matisse was to increase those risks in *Reclining Nude II* and *III* in 1927 and 1929.

By lengthening and stylizing his sculptures to the point of abstracting the features of the face, by eliminating the expressive anecdote, he brought out the contradiction of a body in repose but under tension, whose model he admired in Michaelangelo's *Dawn*, lying at the feet of Lorenzo de Medici.

Luxe I, 1907
Oil on canvas, 210 x 138 cm
*Musée national d'Art moderne,
Paris*

Luxe I

Matisse painted two
versions of Luxe, one with
a realistic treatment
Luxe I, the other
decorative, *Luxe II*. This
parallel treatment of the
same theme, which is
frequent in his work,
is proof of the conflict
between, as he put it,
"sculptural plastic art" and
"colored plastic art".
Here he uses the
procedure, which we have
already seen in *Luxe,
calme et volupté*, of the
transposition of a crayon
drawing to the canvas.
This technique allowed
him to fill in the
compartments of color in
the manner of Puvis de
Chavannes. The
composition in stages from
close to distant by means
of planes of different
colors remained a constant
of the imaginary outdoor
scenes painted by Matisse
during this period and is
similar to Gauguin.
At the same moment when
Matisse reached an almost
Expressionist apotheosis of
colors with *Blue Nude
(Souvenir of Biskra)*, he
explored the effects of an
art where the number was
reduced; here three or
four, whose shades are

bruised, drawn towards ochres.

Luxe I is part of a series of paintings on the theme of idleness and pleasure which ran from 1907 to 1911: bathers, bowls players, dancers and musicians, nymphs and satyrs in an increasingly abstract setting. It may also be considered a monumental fragment of the characters on the shore in *Luxe, calme et volupté* and a foreshadowing of the decor of *Dance*. The greatness of a painter lies in his capacity to generate new myths rooted in ancient ones. The theme of *Luxe* also finds resonances in the myth of the Golden Age of the Greek poets, brought back to life by Ingres and the artists of the late 19th century. But it was Matisse who transposed the myth into the context of a profane scene: drying after a bathe heightens the emotional impact of the unexpected action of a naked girl running to show the bouquet she has picked, whose color and arabesque draw the eye to the other girl's hair, depicting a love which has more to do with the family virtues than the perverse innocence of the Hellenic gods.

LA SERPENTINE, 1909
Bronze, hauteur :
56.5 x 28 x 19 cm
*The Museum of Modern Art (Gift
of Alby Aldrich Rockefeller),
New York*

LA SERPENTINE

Matisse did about sixty
sculptures, most of them
from two periods, 1900-
1911 and 1923-1930. This
one, sculpted in the studio
at Issy-les-Moulineaux, is
the apogee of the first
period.
"I took some clay," wrote
Matisse, "to give myself a
rest from painting, as I had
done absolutely everything
I could do with it for the
time being." Indeed,
sculpture also enriched his
research into two-
dimensional forms by
allowing him to try them
out in three dimensions. In
this respect, *La Serpentine*,
which came between the
two versions of *Dance*
(1909 and 1910), shows
how he used the torsion,
the arabesque, and the
distortions of the bent leg
of the sculpture in the
second version.
By this time Matisse had
distanced himself from the
influence of Rodin. He
constructed his sculpture
in hollows and searched
for the play of
contradictory forces
behind the forms; here the
solid anchorage of a
disproportionate foot on
the ground is in opposition
to the lifting of the other.
Thus, *La Serpentine* may
be read both as a pause and
a dance step.
The pause comes from
the model in the
photograph that Matisse
used for his sculpture.
A plump young woman
whom he stripped of
flesh, though he kept a

realistic representation of
her way of crossing her
legs, of arching her back,
of thrusting out her torso
by folding one arm behind
her back, and leaning the
other elbow on a table, a
finger in her sulky mouth.
The dance step is in the
line that marks the pause
and whose opposing
curves trace arabesques.
Pierre Schneider neatly
said that in his sculptures
Matisse operated
"a daphneisation, the
transformation of the
human form into vegetable
matter." Woman-stalk or
woman-liana, resting on
the trunk of a mineralized
tree, *La Serpentine*
reminds us that in 1907
Douanier Rousseau
showed *The Snake
Charmer,* but above and
beyond the symbol of
paradise, Matisse's
sculpture refers back to an
image of woman which is
more Mannerist than
Naive, more modern than
primitive. In that respect
it heralds the transparent
sculpture of Lipchitz,
Zadkine, and Giacometti.

THE DESSERT:
A HARMONY IN RED, 1908
Oil on canvas, 180 x 220 cm
The Hermitage Museum,
St. Petersburg

THE DESSERT: A HARMONY IN RED

Matisse's style can be read
as an art of minimal
perspective, an art
of purely decorative color,
as a language of plastic
signs.
Perspective is expressed
first of all by the
construction of retreating
lines (for the chair, the
table, the window frame,
the little house); then by
successive planes of color
– red, green, blue – at the

level of the window; lastly
by the illusion of
perspective which makes
us interpret the curve of
the arabesque on the cloth
in the foreground as a fold,
the part where it falls
towards the floor.
But Matisse limits the
perspective; he makes
elisions in the line around
the table, frames the
chair, the window, and
the little house in an
innovative manner by
cutting them off, and
encloses two of the planes,

the green and the blue, in
the window.
*The Dessert: A Harmony
in Red* went through three
successive stages. First it
was green, then blue, after
it was hung at the Salon
d'Automne in 1908. It was
finally delivered in scarlet
to the Russian collector
Shchukin to decorate his
dining room.
The single background
color allows the eye to rest
and confers a sense of
unreality on the other
colors which, afloat in a

weightless space, function as abstract elements. Van Gogh and Gauguin had integrated the arabesque into their decorative period. The landscape in the window and the modern treatment of the dining room are the mark of a combination of color and arabesque peculiar to Matisse, notably through the thick blue shading of the stalks of the flowers. If we set these plastic elements alongside the one formed by the maid, a kind of effigy in the style of turn-of-the-century advertisements, we see that Matisse works on his forms by cutting them up in the color with a brush as he was to do later with the scissors.

The naive, imaginary landscape in the window refers us to a hidden meaning: the myth of the Garden of Eden or the suggested presence of another member of the family, the child we find again in Gauguin's *Monsieur Loulou*, which is very close to the handling of this landscape.

DANCE, 1910
Oil on canvas, 260 x 391 cm
*The Hermitage Museum,
St. Petersburg*

DANCE

Matisse's *Dance* and
Picasso's *Guernica* are the
cult works of the 20th
century. *Dance* symbolizes
freedom and unity;
Guernica is the memory
of horror.
Matisse's and Picasso's
works are also close in
their execution. While
Matisse painted *La Joie de
Vivre* in 1906, expressing
the myth of Eden through
Art Nouveau and colored

abstraction, Picasso
responded in 1907 with
*Les Demoiselles
d'Avignon*, a painting of
whores in Cubist style. A
zoom to one of the scenes
of the pleasure garden,
Dance shows that Picasso
did not hold an exclusive
on modernity.
Picasso went to the
brothel, and so Matisse
went to the music hall and
watched the farandole of
the dancers: "I have
composed my dance...
singing the same tune I
had heard at the Moulin de
la Galette so that the whole
composition, all the
dancers, are in time and
dancing to the same
rhythm." But if the rhythm
creates the union of the

bodies, it also transforms
the representation of the
female body through
movement. Picasso the
Cubist reconstructed
planes piece by piece;
Matisse the decorative
artist reconstructs by
speed. To the stop-frame
image of the
Impressionists, he opposes
cinematographic
decomposition, which
brings out the torsion of
each limb. The feminine
bodies of Renoir's bathers
are followed by the virile
bodies of Matisse's
dancers. The imaginary
chain of bodies of *Dance*,
which sprang from the
*Combat of Greeks and
Amazons* (5th century
B.C.) and the *Young*

Women exercising at the Games from the mosaics of Roman villas (2nd century B.C.) meets the athletes of the 1900 Olympic Games in Paris. The dance was to be body-building before it became body art.
It also links up with the expressionist painting of Greek vases (420-380 B.C.); layering the figures in depth, absence of decorative overload, dramatization of the gestures of the hands reaching out for one another, leaving a gap with a place for a sixth dancer: the viewer?
Lastly, a restricted range of colors: "A beautiful blue for the sky," said Matisse, "... the green of the hill and the scarlet of the bodies."
But the intensity of the colors, the frontal language of the drawings, the reduction of the nude to a united red plane, and the work's resemblance to a backdrop silenced the critics at the Salon d'Automne in 1910.
As for Shchukin, he announced that the nudes might shock his nieces and then hung the picture in his townhouse in Moscow.

MUSIC, 1910
Oil on canvas, 260 x 389 cm
The Hermitage Museum,
St. Petersburg

MUSIC

After *Dance*, *Music* is the
second panel of
Shchukin's commission to
decorate his town house in
Moscow. "On the second
floor," wrote Matisse,
"you are inside the house,
inside its spirit and its
silence; I see a musical
scene with people
listening." Rediscovering
certain intuitions of
Mallarmé writing about

mime: "Silence in the
afternoons of music, how
pleased I am to find it, too,
at the always original
entrance of Pierrot,"
Matisse creates an allegory
of music made of the
silence of naked bodies
miming musicians and
singers, rather like Pierrot
Lunaire.
Photos of *Music* in
progress show that Matisse
had first painted a more
realistic scene, close to the
Bathers with Turtle and
Musique Esquisse, with a
dog, figures face to face in
profile, and flowers.
That elimination of
anecdotal elements
signifies the painter's wish
for purification.
Music thus rediscovers the

principles of figuration of
Christian (frescoes from
the Synagogue of Doura
Europos) or Byzantine
art: the absence of
plasticity, the unnatural
gestures, the lightness of
the figures brushing the
ground as if in a state of
weightlessness, the
absence of a border
from the stretch of space
around the figures, the
sketchiness of forms and
signs, the diaphanousness
of pictorial material.
But Matisse's procedure is
not like that of the
Christian artists inspired
by Plotinus in search of a
mystical fusion. With the
poem *Un coup de dés
jamais n'abolira le hasard*
(A throw of the dice will

never abolish chance), Mallarmé had created a new literary space by giving the reader a multiplicity of possible readings. Similarly, Matisse constructs a new pictorial space founded on series of plastic signs (blocks of red of the bodies, black punctuation of the faces) and an aleatory way of parcelling out the forms: variability in the spacing and the ordering of signs in the ranging of the characters, who no longer form a geometrical pattern as in *Dance*; and variability of temporal references through the Pan pipes and the modern violin. Matisse did not know that Schönberg would bring about a similar revolution in music some years later, or that another music would take up the organized violence and worldliness of his pictorial gesture: jazz.

**VIEW OF COLLIOURE AND
THE SEA,** 1911
Oil on canvas, 61 x 49.6 cm
*The Museum of Modern Art
(Nelson A. Rockefeller Bequest),
New York*

VIEW OF COLLIOURE AND THE SEA

From 1900 to 1911 Matisse's work is particularly fertile in landscapes painted from nature. First done with Impressionist handling (*Path, Bois de Boulogne*, 1902), the landscapes passed through Fauvism to the purest abstraction (*Landscape at Collioure*, 1905), before returning to more realistic representations. *View of Collioure* from 1911 reaches a balance rarely achieved between the Impressionist rendering of the changeable weather, the Cézanne-like construction of the landscape and the Expressionism of the color.

The sky looks as if it had been painted by Renoir or Sisley: a fluid, whirling touch, slightly graduated shades, the misshapen appearance of the branches of the trees which expresses the force of the wind. Nevertheless, the colored shadows of the branches, treated like abstract silhouettes in the manner of Gauguin, introduce a feeling of strangeness. Matisse wrote: "A Sisley is a moment of nature, a Cézanne is a moment of the artist." It is indeed to Cézanne that we owe the manner of

framing a landscape with a great tree (*Mont Sainte-Victoire with a Large Pine Tree*), and of deviating the perpendiculars. The black line that splits the picture obliquely breaks the right-angle formed by the tree and the horizon. And a Cézanne-style construction in the geometrical volume of the houses and the choice of an overhead perspective in the foreground; a tilt brought back on balance by a second elevated plane (the church tower).

The picture is read from top to bottom, which reinforces the succession of colors, alternately warm and cold, streaks of light and color.

But in the end it is the figurative period of Kandinsky, with Expressionist canvases like *Landscape with Houses*, that this work reminds us of.

With Matisse, landscape underwent its third pictorial revolution. The Renaissance discovered distances; the 19th century the variability of the vision of nature under the influence of the weather. Matisse shows that a landscape is also a set of intense colorings which find their echo in us regardless of our recognition of forms.

THE CONVERSATION,
1909-1912
Oil on canvas, 177 x 217 cm
The Hermitage Museum,
St. Petersburg

THE CONVERSATION

This canvas is composed like certain 15th century paintings that Matisse had seen on his journey to Italy in 1907: a central opening in a wall, characters in profile forming a diptych, and a solemn air which recalls the Duke and Duchess of Urbino in the painting by Piero della Francesca. However, Matisse does not open a window onto the exterior; he closes the perspective. Following the path taken by Gauguin in 1889 with *The Yellow Christ* and *Self-Portrait,* he creates images with flat figures on a monochrome background (here a blue which is reminiscent of Giotto) and paints the distances in the non-realist style of the early Renaissance.

In fact, *The Conversation* treats the garden of the Matisse house in Issy-les-Moulineaux as a backdrop of geometrical forms; the flower-beds recall the Art Deco Mannerist motifs of Gustav Klimt. But Matisse is not content to paint a backdrop instead of a view: the closed window of his studio at the bottom of the garden, the same blue as the room, symbolically repeats the decorative use of the opening.

The effigy effect of the characters is reinforced by

the verticals of the stripes of the pyjamas, the slab of black of the dressing gown, the immaterial air of the paste, and the brilliant invention of an armchair without pictorial matter. In this way Matisse contributes to the creation of new two-dimensional virtual images, and we understand his jubilation on seeing the Russian icons on his journey to Moscow in late 1911.

These images find their meaning in a renewed code of interpretation of the world: no longer to the glory of princes as in the Renaissance, nor to the heroes of the profane or religious myths of the 19th-century, but to the modern family. Matisse in pyjamas and his wife in a dressing gown are the symbol of a century in which the 19th-century wall of private life was blown to smithereens, when man and woman would come face to face like two beings with distinct identities. Before the theoreticians of the psychology of forms and after Freud's studies of the "family novel," Matisse inscribed the difference between the sexes in the opposition of colors (black/blue, red/green) and lines (vertical/curved) which are repeated from one motif of the painting to another.

FLOWERS AND CERAMICS, 1911
Oil on canvas, 93.5 x 82.5 cm
*Städelsches Kunstinstitut und
Städtische Galerie, Frankfurt*

FLOWERS AND CERAMICS

In his still lifes Matisse tries out some formal research which he takes up again in his other genres: portraits, interiors, nudes. This picture marks the change from a decorative style, which assigns an important part to the arabesque and the patterns on fabrics, to a more abstract one.

The room with the still life appears in 1910 in *Still Life with Geraniums*; we see a realistic version of the panelled walls and the slatted wooden floor. Here the effect of depth is neutralized by the use of a single color applied in large brush strokes to the floor and the wall, and yet maintained by the shadow of the flowers on the floor, the folded corner motif, and the black strip, which

also produces the rolling effect of the ball.
Cézanne's *Still Life with Cherub* (1895) had already used similar effects.
In Matisse's work, blue contrasted with black represents the light/darkness, interior/exterior duality. It reappears in a number of works, such as *Goldfish and Palette*

(1914), in the guise of inserted abstract planes. The flowers (nasturtiums) often crop up in the paintings from 1911. Matisse said, "Flowers provide the best lessons in color composition, (they) often give me impressions of colors which remain indelibly marked on my retina, like a red-hot iron."

The flowers in *Flowers and Ceramics* are blotches of color, some echoing the sphere in a proliferation of subdued blue-green, and others, crimson and violet yellow, creating a new manner of expressing depth by the contrast between them.
The ceramic ball and the open cylinder are imaginary forms probably derived from ceramic objects (cups, plates) used in other works. In Matisse's work, before the Surrealists, the object is used as the zero degree of a language of colored forms. *Flowers and Ceramics* is thus composed from a real object, the flowers, and a zero object, the ball, which floats unreally in a space which has lost its usual references of depth and weight and seems to be animated by a whirling movement. The two green balls rolling on a red plane in *Purple Cyclamen*, painted in the same year, confirm Matisse's interest in unusual forms.

THE RED STUDIO, 1911
Oil on canvas, 181 x 219.1 cm
*The Museum of Modern Art
(Mrs Simon Guggenheim Fund),
New York*

THE RED STUDIO

The Red Studio is both an intimate, personal room in a bourgeois house – as in Vuillard's work – and an art studio; that is to say, a place where the decor and its objects are as important as the painter and his model in the studios of the 19th century. The decor here consists of a happy jumble of objects, assembled more from affection than consideration for style. The paintings, the ceramic plate, and the sculptures are by Matisse; they span the Fauve period from *Marin II* (1906) to *Purple Cyclamen* (1911). The works play the part of decorative images; the frames of the pictures are neutralized by a decor with floral motifs.
The painter's tools are captured in the midst of unusual functions: the crayons like still lifes beside the knives, the stools like furniture beside the chest of drawers, the frames with their canvases like surfaces waiting to be colored like the wall. To the left of the picture we can see a rectangle which is still unpainted, or rather painted pale blue, the first color of the work.
The furniture and the decanter are not functional; they live in a space which is for play – they are the painter's actors – and in a time which cannot be measured, as symbolized by the clock without hands.
In *The Red Studio* Matisse is not painting the artist at work like Courbet, nor the other side of the decor like the painters of the 1970s, but the decorative work itself.
To do so he creates a new plastic language, close to Oriental art on metal, the result of which is to be seen in the red copper plaque of an engraving of a studio whose hollows have not yet been filled with ink. A language which is also an art of transparence and the superimposition of matter and which, during the same period, Picasso, Delaunay, and Braque were seeking through Cubism. But, at the same time, a language of the dispersion of signs on a flat surface which does not allow the eye to rest, also inherited from the Orient, and which, from Miró to the graffiti on city walls, is the language of the decorative art of today.

**ZORAH ON THE
TERRACE,** 1912-1913
Oil on canvas, 116 x 80 cm
Pushkin Museum, Moscow

ZORAH ON THE TERRACE

When Matisse disembarked at Tangier in January 1912, it was raining. The rain lasted a month; when the sun came out it gave him an aesthetic shock. "The light is so gentle, quite different from the Mediterranean," he wrote.

The differently colored geometrical surfaces of the picture are the transcription of a cutting up of space by effects of shadow and light which are felt rather than perceived. The pink triangle is a sunlit surface, the blue represents the penumbra which slides from the wall to Zorah and from Zorah to the floor, cutting out a parallelepiped. But the penumbra is determined in relation to the shadow: the carpet. The effect of fluidity and transparence is created by the superimposition of dabs of an almond blue-green on a pink background. In the heat, objects lose their solidity, they become mirages; all at once the ring that marked out their

borders is reduced until it vanishes or inverts itself, creating a state of levitation which culminates in the slippers placed on the pure penumbra. The face, with its ochre-yellow color, reduced to a few lines, expresses calm, an emotion underlined by the pose – the figure seated on folded legs – which allows Matisse to enclose a human body in the shape of a vase.

The figure of Zorah is treated like the Persian miniatures that Matisse had admired at the Munich exhibition in 1910. In Tangier he asked his Moroccan models to wear their traditional costumes, whose accessories allowed him to heighten the colors of the decorative motifs; here the red of the sash and the yellow points of the embroidery of the jellaba. But they are effaced by the white and blue geometrical motif of the tunic, more in keeping with the young girl's virginal appearance.

The proliferation of objects in *The Red Studio* contrasts with the emptiness of the space in the Moroccan works. In *Zorah on the Terrace,* the goldfish and the golden slippers are symbols of the Orient. They are used to construct a kind of allegory of beauty and modesty. The slippers create a visual link between Zorah and the fish; they are at once ornaments by their arabesque motif and fish by their red color and oval shape. Thus Zorah, her beauty modestly covered by her tunic, is presented to our gaze on her carpet in a globe of light, like goldfish in their bowl.

INTERIOR,
GOLDFISH BOWL, 1914
Oil on canvas, 147 x 97 cm
Musée national d'Art moderne,
Paris

INTERIOR, GOLDFISH BOWL

This painting brings
together three of Matisse's
favorite motifs: the studio,
the window, the goldfish.
The studio is the one on
the Quai Saint-Michel; it
occurs again in a similar
composition in several
paintings of the period, in
particular, in *The Studio in
the Quai Saint-Michel* and
*The Painter and his
Model.* Matisse juxtaposes
three angles of vision here:
an overhead perspective on
the table, the ceramic
plate, and the armchair in
the foreground; a view in
approaching the plane of
the rest of the room,
misshapen as if by a wide-
angle lens which draws the
eye towards the bowl and
its stand and stretches out
the opening of the
window; an image of the
Palais de Justice which
turns it into a painted
backdrop like the one
Masaccio used in the 15th
century to represent
Florence in the
Resurrection of Tabitha

and *Healing of the Sick.*
The light outside is unreal,
like the stage lighting in a
theatre or the lamps used
to light a day-for-night
scene in a film. A midnight
blue filter which, with the
black of the floor and
the gray of the furniture,
evokes the war and refers
to an artistic movement
which was working with
more sober colors at the
time: Cubism. *Goldfish
and Palette* (1914-1915)
was the Cubist version of
Interior, Goldfish Bowl.
The goldfish bowl, a large
laboratory jar, has no
accessories and the water
is perfectly limpid. That
transparence is already to
be found in the 1911
Goldfish, where the image,
doubled by the reflection
on the surface of the
water, reinforces
the decorative effect.
Here the fish represent the
model, her absence evoked
by the red mark on the
divan; while the goldfish
bowl and the pot of
flowers by the window are
no less emblematic of the
painter's work. Between
the still life they compose
and the backdrop of the
Palais de Justice and
the Seine behind the
window, only art can build
bridges. From the
flowerpot, lines of black
ink sprout and merge
with the black stains on
the quays – perhaps
passers-by – and the blue-
painted surface of the
water in the bowl plunges
into the Seine. Matisse
thus introduces us to a
metaphysical reflection on
the relations between
nature, the artist, and
artificial life, which he
often discussed at the time
with Prichard in
the intellectual and
mystical milieu of Sarah
Stein's drawing room.

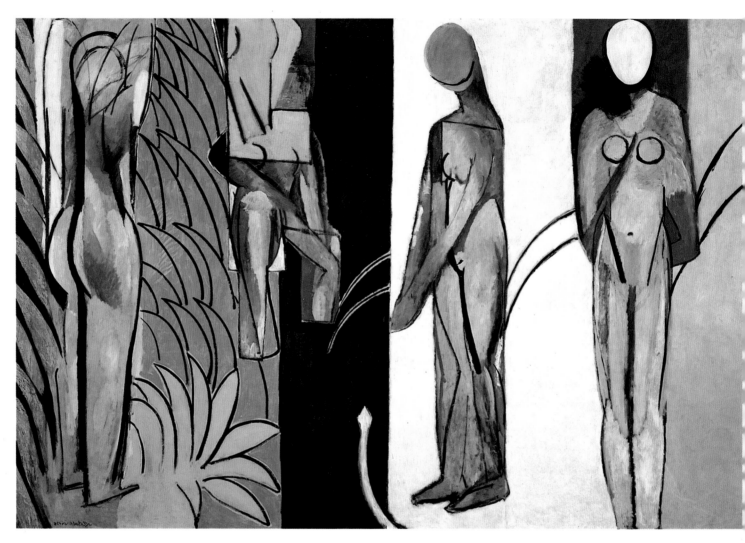

BATHERS BY A RIVER, 1916
Oil on canvas, 259.7 x 389.9 cm
*The Art Institute (Charles H. et
Mary F.S. Worcester Collection),
Chicago*

BATHERS BY A RIVER

According to Pierre
Schneider, the idea for this
painting was proposed by
Matisse to Shchukin as the
third panel of a triptych,
with *Dance* and *Music*.
They were all begun
during that period, but
probably abandoned for
want of a commission and
returned to in 1913 in a
style where geometry takes
pride of place over color,
linking up with the
investigations which
marked the evolution from
Cubism to abstraction and
which he was engaged in
at the time with Juan Gris
in Collioure.
The division of the picture
into four vertical strips
prevents any reading in
depth and constitutes a
sequence of planes which
are read in succession with
a single reference for
interpretation: the
vegetation on the river
bank. This kind of
sequential organization is
not found again until
Dance for Barnes at
Merion, completed in
1933, though in the late
sixties it generated an art
of sequence painting with
Andy Warhol.
Here the sequence is
animated by the induced
dynamism of the figures: a
single human body, seen
from different angles and
distances, performs a
simultaneous movement of
rotation and elevation

before our eyes. The rotation is expressed by a decomposition of movements operated by a displacement of color and the line of the limbs of the two central figures. The elevation appears in the representation of the busts and arms of the same figures, which superimpose two views at two different distances; a procedure implicit in the figures on the right, more marked on the next body and becoming the object of a cut superimposed on the seated figure. Lastly, the abstract line in the shape of a leaf, which runs from right to left and top to bottom, suggests the possibility of the superimposition of different panels.

The bodies seem to have been worked in a clay bas-relief from which they have retained an earth color. *Bathers by a River* displays an indecency of flesh color which we find in Soutine and which reappeared later in Bacon and Velickovic. The eroticism is reinforced by the anonymous oval of the faces, by the particular lighting of a breast or a belly, and by the life of the line itself – as if Matisse was drawing over a painting to create a collage of lines and colors. The symbol of temptation, the serpent – a water snake – brings into the Matissian paradise of bliss something of the lust of Picasso's *Demoiselles d'Avignon*. Through representation, the female body has become an art object.

THE PIANO LESSON, 1916
Oil on canvas, 245.1 x 212.7 cm
*The Museum of Modern Art
(Mrs Simon Guggenheim Fund),
New York*

THE PIANO LESSON

The Music Lesson (1917)
and *The Piano Lesson* are
two interpretations of the
same reality: the
interpenetration of art and
family life. *The Piano
Lesson* is like the sketch,
the idea; *The Music
Lesson* is the expression
of the feeling. They stand
in contrast in rather the
same way that
W. Worringer in 1918
described the evolution of
art as the alternation of a
need for geometrical
abstraction (Gothic style)
and a need for *einfülung*,
or empathy (the
naturalistic style of
the Renaissance).
Matisse found the theme
in Fragonard when he
copied *The Music Lesson*
around 1890.
But *The Piano Lesson*
does not derive so much
from Fragonard as from
Vuillard who, in *The
Piano* (1896), had painted
a bourgeois scene where
the decor, charged with
floral motifs and the
family atmosphere,
seemed to smother the
music. Vuillard's work is
reassuring; Matisse's is
disturbing, worrying even.
The Piano Lesson is
indeed one of those rare
"Vanities" of modern
painting, one of those 17th
century still lifes that
presented through certain
symbolic objects a
metaphysical reflection on
time, art, and death.

Time is present in the
metronome and the candle,
but also in the fact that
Matisse has deliberately
made his son Pierre,
sitting at the piano,
younger, referring us back
to the time when he took
him out of high school so
that he could learn an
instrument. The presence
of the triangular gray
shadow on the child's face
includes it in a repertoire
of symbolic forms and
objects, perhaps a sundial.
This subject is a synthesis
of the arts practized by
Matisse: the woman sitting
in the background is
Woman and Stool (1914)
and the sculpture is
Decorative Figure (1908).
Here the two works are
reduced to their rough
draft. But it is also the
decorative style of the
arabesque, the ones on the
balcony forming heart-
shaped traceries and the
ones on the piano where
the word PLEYEL is read
back-to-front like mirror
writing; it is also the
musical style of the color
where the gentle, bright
shades of the red of the
piano, the green of the
garden and the orange of
the wall seem to be forces
of resistance in one of the
most austere universes
created by Matisse, made
of triangles and angles.
The presence of death, too,
for if the music can sound
in this space where the
anecdotal family element
is kept to a minimum (the
child's head) and where no
decoration is allowed to
muffle the sounds, it has a
lugubrious sonority which
bounces off the purely
abstract opacity of the
exterior landscape and
the neutrality of the
walls invaded by the
gray shadow of
the 1914-1918 war.

**VIOLINIST AT THE
WINDOW,** 1918
Oil on canvas, 150 x 98 cm
*Musée national d'Art moderne,
Paris*

VIOLINIST AT THE WINDOW

Matisse, a passionate
amateur violinist, was one
of a number of painter
musicians of the 1900s:
Douanier Rousseau,
Redon, Vlaminck, Klee.
Violinist at the Window is
an evocation of Matisse
himself.
From the *Guitarist* in 1903
to *Jazz* in 1943, music is
intimately involved with
the evolution of his work.
With *Interior with Violin,
Violinist at the Window*,
painted in the same year,
marked a return by the
painter to an aesthetic
where emotional
experience once again
animates the lines and
colors; an aesthetic present
in *The Music Lesson* in
1917.
The window is open onto a
landscape where the
harmony of the hues of
dawn echoes the peaceful
state of mind of the person
playing. The black and
white of the days of
anxiety, relegated to the
area around the window,
nevertheless show that the
wounds of the years 1914-
1918 have not yet healed,
for the country or the
family. However, after the
angular geometry which
dominates *The Piano
Lesson*, the curve resumes
its role as counterpoint in
the figure and the
landscape, while the
straight line is stabilized in
a perfect symmetry
animated only by the
oblique of the bow which
creates the depth.
The figure has become a

sign again, as in *Music*; a sign which refers not to an immemorial, primitive rite but to a new, more modern archetype of the musician. In those same years, Chagall was pursuing the soul of the violinist in Hassidic folklore with a wealth of color which Matisse would not have disowned. They both endow their characters with that fragility of the artist faced with the world of men and the city, which is still asleep here. A fragility rendered by the rising perspective of the floor, the overhanging effect of the clouds and sky and the unexpected touch of the chin-rest falling over the back. And the elegance of the violin: Matisse – unlike Picasso or Braque who decomposed it with their cut-and-paste – always preserved the integrity of its form; and its notes seem to have colored the sky.

An atypical work, in the end *Violinist at the Window* is a trailer for the strip cartoons of the forties, a "Tintin on the Riviera," where Matisse would be spending all his winters in the future.

WHITE FEATHERS, 1919
Oil on canvas, 70.3 x 60.3 cm
*The Institute of Arts (The William
Hood Dunwoody Fund),
Minneapolis*

WHITE FEATHERS

Woman in a Hat had
marked the apogee of
Matisse's Fauve period
and *White Feathers* opens
the Nice period.
With this picture, Matisse
is effectively breaking
with the severe
geometrical style of the
portraits of the war years,
such as those of Sarah
Stein, Greta Prozor, or
Auguste Pellerin, which
tended to reduce the
face to an icon. Here he
returns to the art of the
realistic portrait, which he
had practiced in his years
of apprenticeship at the
École des Beaux-Arts and
his copies at the Louvre.
White Feathers thus
renews the great tradition
of the princely portrait
which, from Van Eyck to
Dürer and from the 15th
century to Raphael, was
passed on to Ingres in
the 19th century. The
influence of Ingres, which
was much in fashion in
artistic circles at the time,

s to be seen in Derain or Picasso (*Portrait of Olga in an Armchair,* 1917). The uniform red background, slightly darker on the left – as if there might be a space for a *veduta* – the alabaster texture of the dress, the mother-of-pearl of the flesh, and the flamboyance of the ostrich feather give the portrait a haughty air which brings it close to the portraits of the Renaissance. Nevertheless, Matisse does not paint the feathers with the same minute detail as Dürer painted the fur in *Portrait of a Young Man* (1521), and the features of the face do not have the smooth, close-grained handling of Ingres in the portrait of *Baroness James de Rothschild* (1848). If the face is thus somewhat lacking in soul, the color contrast shows that Matisse is once again concerned with light. *White Feathers* is not a portrait of a member of his family or a close friend as his earlier portraits were. This is a model, Antoinette, whom he has disguised for the circumstances and of whom he did some of his most beautiful drawings. The hat, made by the painter himself, reminds us of his interest in the world of fashion. The choice of a music-hall feather, the addition of the fantastic dangling ornaments of the hat, the cheap emerald broach, the carelessly bared shoulder, and the slightly tantalizing expression show that Matisse had not lost his taste for the provocative. The Baroque Matisse takes an ironic look at the Classical Matisse.

WOMAN AND GOLDFISH, 1921
Oil on canvas, 81 x 100 cm
*The Art Institute (Helen Birch
Bartlett Memorial Collection),
Chicago*

WOMAN AND GOLDFISH

Matisse discovered the theme of people looking at goldfish in 1912 in the cafés of Tangier. He wrote, "I had my bowl of fish and my pink flower and what struck me was those big devils that stand for hours staring at a flower and a bowl of goldfish!" After *The Arab Café* (1913), where a group of Moroccans are squatting on the floor staring at a bowl of goldfish, he took up the theme again in 1921 with two intimate versions of the same scene: one prosaic, *Woman looking at an Aquarium*, the other magical, *Woman and Goldfish*.

In *Woman and Goldfish,* Matisse takes as a background a motif from Arab architecture, the latticework often used by the Orientalist painters (Lewis, *The Siesta*, 1876). That transparent, repetitive, geometrical figure allows him both to suggest a volume beyond the picture and to create the effect of a decorative surface. The woman and the goldfish bowl would be just motifs on a backdrop if the two bars, green and blue, did not keep the latticework away from the surface of the painting, and if the table in sloping perspective did not draw the young woman and the objects towards the foreground.

The technique of figuration of reality used by Matisse is quite different from Renoir or Manet. Indeed the modelling of the face or the bowl is not rendered by a gradation of colors but by the addition of white. The water in the bowl loses in translucence but gains in mystery; the fish themselves have shed their red color for a chameleonic black, orange-red, and yellow. Pierre Schneider said that

Woman and Goldfish is one of the most accomplished works of "chromatic Surrealism." That Surrealism is reinforced by the slabs of color which spill over their outlines – the model's hair is the same color as the surround of the armchair, and the pink of the table is identical to the pink of the arm – and by the treatment of the branches of pine cones, garlands painted flush with the table or against the young

girl's arm.
The theme of contemplation led Matisse to make the daydream one of his favorite subjects. This indolent young woman, languid and dreamy, who is sunk in contemplation of a goldfish bowl as if it were a crystal ball, is one of the rare images of the woman-child in the work of Matisse. We have to wait for Balthus to find young girls gazing questioningly at themselves in mirrors.

DECORATIVE FIGURE ON AN ORNAMENTAL BACKGROUND, 1925
Oil on canvas, 130 x 98 cm
Musée national d'Art moderne, Paris

DECORATIVE FIGURE ON AN ORNAMENTAL BACKGROUND

At once Classical and Baroque, realistic and decorative, this painting is a paradoxical work. At the Salon des Tuileries in 1926, some critics vituperated Matisse's Orientalist bad taste, while others saw in it his return to stable Western values. For some years Matisse had been searching among the works of the Italian Renaissance – in the sculptures of Donatello or Michaelangelo – for the decorative effect of a volume.

In some of his sculptures (*Seated Venus*, 1918, or *Venus with Shell*, 1930), as with the figure in the picture, the anatomy is made of interlocking volumes: the oval of the head, the cylinders of the trunk and the limbs. The abrupt construction of the body, as if it had been hacked out with an axe, may have inspired Picasso in his Surrealistic representation of the *Bather Opening a Cabin* (1928). Picasso had also taken a detour around Michaelangelo (*The Pan Pipes*, 1923).

The Michaelangelo aspect can be clearly seen if we frame the body at the level of the fabric falling from the back to the thigh and the backdrop, keeping the oblique black lines which mark the perspective on the floor. The decor is one of the most heavily laden and heterogeneous in the work of Matisse: French Baroque wall paper, Venetian Rococo mirror, Oriental flower pot, Persian carpet. The accumulation is reminiscent of the interiors of Vuillard, with the difference that here the pictorial treatment also varies from one style to another: Fauvism in the frame of the mirror, use of the arabesque in the pattern of the carpet and the wallpaper, Pointillism on the cushion, Impressionism in the oranges, Cubist and African lines of the face. The abundance of signifieds and signifiers also disturbs any classical reading of the work and keeps the eye constantly on the move, impelled also by the central illusion effect of the canvas which swings the figure backwards and forwards between real object and decorative element and the decor between three-dimensional reality and two-dimensional abstraction. Matisse has thus laid optical traps for his audience. When the eye moves away from the figure, its uncertainty increases; the carpet, with its arabesques, and the flower pot form a single body with the wallpaper; the floral motif on the left seems to be a bloom on the orange tree.

Decorative Figure on an Ornamental Background thus maintains two antinomic aesthetics in an unstable balance: the interlocking volumetric forms, which we also find in the figures of Fernand Léger, and the decorative illusion which creates a *trompe-l'œil* and undoes it at the same time.

ODALISQUE WITH GRAY TROUSERS, 1927
Oil on canvas, 54 x 65 cm
Musée de l'Orangerie, Paris

ODALISQUE WITH GRAY TROUSERS

The theme of the odalisque arises both from Matisse's attraction towards Oriental art and from his memories of his journeys to Morocco, as well as his taste for the light and the cosmopolitan world of the Riviera in the years after the war.
The word "odalisque" was used by the Turks to designate the sultan's handmaiden, "oda" meaning bedroom. Representation of the odalisque in the 19th century evolved from the montage of a Europeanized courtesan in an Empire setting to the Arab woman in a harem with Oriental decor. In *Odalisque with Gray Trousers* Matisse parodies those references by giving free rein to plays of color and forms in which the female body occupies a central place.
"Take a good look at those odalisques," he wrote "in that atmosphere of languid relaxation, in the torpor of that sunlight which bathes things and beings, a great tension is brewing, of a specifically pictorial order, a tension which emerges from the interplay and the interrelations of the elements."
That tension is first presented in the very construction of the space of the picture, which associates a classical

perspective – the divan and the striped cushion on which the odalisque is reclining in a style so reminiscent of *The Grand Odalisque* by Ingres – with an ambivalent view of the fabric in the foreground, which is at once a bed and a wall hanging, and the hanging on the right, painted in *trompe-l'œil*.

The tension is then created by the multiplication of decorative motifs: vertical streaks, cross-pieces, and arabesques, which clash on the surface and in depth.

Lastly, the alternation in the foreground of bright and subdued colors – red and pale pink, light grey and dark green – and the alternating repetition of colors and white in the stripes of the wallpaper, create an optical and kinetic effect which heralds the investigations of Vasarely.

Here, the drawing of the body blends into the cushion at the feet; there, its curves contrast with the vertical lines.

The body is no longer a plastic whole; it is a composition of multiple graphic signs: the black lines of the mouth and the eyes, the red touches of the breasts, the arrow of the foot, in contradiction with, or emerging from, the unselfconsciousness of the pose.

Matisse makes the eroticism visible by means of a new language of the line and color of the body; it is no longer modest, but voluptuous – sensual even when athletic. A body which has lost that childlike, wild creature candor of Renoir's odalisques, a little awkward beneath the finery of the "Algerian woman," and which poses for the pleasure of the person looking and painting.

The light which bathes the whole composition gives the impression of a beach scene among the bathing huts, the canvas of the deck chairs, and the colored towels, a holiday atmosphere in a joyful post-war year.

ODALISQUE WITH TURKISH ARMCHAIR, 1928
Oil on canvas, 60 x 73 cm
Musée d'Art moderne de la Ville de Paris

ODALISQUE WITH TURKISH ARMCHAIR

Gustave Moreau built Symbolist Oriental palaces for the Salomes, Cleopatras, or Delilahs of his Romantic readings. Matisse provided modern style Oriental decors for the apartments he imagined for his models. In answer to those who reproached him for abandoning his avant-garde plastic investigations, Matisse wrote, "With the *Odalisques*, I am not giving up what I have just won... but I am returning to a vibration of depth, I am readmitting a certain modelling and repossessing a space where the air begins to circulate. One problem has arisen here: how to harmonize and balance the pure tones and the half-shades."

Here Matisse extinguishes his pure tones with the aid of a cleverly distributed white and accentuates the provocative side of the odalisque by the use of black for the braid of hair, the checkerboard, and the background motifs of the wallpaper.

The Baroque wallpaper, the Jouy fabric with the Persian motif, and the checkerboard, which appear in a number of canvases after 1910, are his plastic equivalent of

rhetorical figures and can represent, with slight modifications, a perspective space or a decorative space; this is particularly the case with the checkerboard and the hangings.

But a new object appears here: the armchair. The chair functioned as an element of perspective in his earlier canvases. The numerous armchairs of the thirties and forties had a decorative function,

whether pushed to the limits in *Woman in an Armchair* or *White and Yellow Background* (1940), or reduced to a sculptural object in *The Rocaille Armchair* (1946). Here the Turkish armchair serves both as a prop for the pose and as a decoration.

The odalisques reveal Matisse's qualities as a stylist; he is engaged in high fashion in the folds of the Turkish trousers

and the arrangement of the blouse and bodice, whose style could well be the subject of a contemporary fashion parade. The composition is a subtle play of forms and colors which are repeated from the body of the odalisque to the objects in the room: the arabesque of the body, the paper, and the cushions, the squares of the checkerboard, and on the belly, the red mark underlining the chest, and

the oval shape of the armchair. The crosswise animation of the picture by the accumulation of open angles creates an invitation to enter the room, an invitation reiterated by the game of checkers which is set for two players.

PINK NUDE, 1935
Oil on canvas, 66 x 92.7 cm
The Museum of Art (The Cone Collection), Baltimore

PINK NUDE

Pink Nude, or *Large Reclining Nude*, follows two events in Matisse's work: the execution of *Dance* for Merion and the illustration of Mallarmé's poems. With those two works, Matisse created new mythical figures in unprecedented plastic spaces: mural painting and book.
Pink Nude belongs to the universe of new forms and ambivalent figures which is contemporary to Surrealism and abstract art. This representation of the female body, sketched in the drawings to illustrate *L'Après-midi d'un Faune*, was to reappear in 1936 in *Nymph in the Forest*.
Pink Nude is thus a metaphor for love: a nymph's body consisting of a heavy, sensual, animal lower part and a more delicate, spiritual human part in the face. The body is not disjointed as it is by the Surrealists, but it is under-jointed by the continuity of the curving line and over-jointed at the level of the head, mobile on the neck but well in place.
In the forties Matisse took photographs of the stages of his work, which he called "the cinema of sensibility." He sent twenty-four photographs to Etta Cone, who was going to buy *Pink Nude*. The first ones show a realistic, conventional interior where a young woman, framed in close up, is lying beside a vase of flowers and a chair. The face is figurative, the body modelled, the chest curved; small squares appear as a background. The evolution of the work

shows first an elongation of the body and more angular limbs, which are reminiscent of Modigliani. The elongation of the female body is also a characteristic of decorative art or the art of the stylists, from the Art Nouveau of Aubrey Beardsley and Gustav Klimt to Art Deco, with the simultaneous dresses of Sonia Delaunay. In other photos, the twisting of the hip caused by the crossed legs and the backward swing of the bust compensated by the exertion of the arm supporting the head give muscle to the body, revealing the influence of *Dawn* by Michaelangelo. In the final version, all the modelling has disappeared. The exertion is reduced to a minimum, the hip is resting flat on the floor, the face is stylized, the chair and the vase have become abstract motifs. The generalization of the chequer pattern and the flattening of the body create a purely decorative effect. The drawing of the body, freed from its dependence on values and color – the color itself is more bruised – marks the borders of the chequered surface, created in the original by strips of pasted paper. The multiplication of "windows" (frames, green squares, white squares) superimposed like the ones on a computer screen, from which the body spills out, reinforces the monumental aspect of the figure in this small-format composition.

Tahiti II

In the early thirties, Matisse made a long journey to the United States and then embarked for Tahiti, where he stayed for three months. Except for his stays in Tangier, his travels were fairly unproductive. Matisse is not a painter of customs or a tourist, and the Tahitian paradise of Gauguin only seduced him on canvas. He had gone in search of new proportions, of non-European space and light, and he returned from Oceania with mixed feelings about a light which was both overwhelming and pure: "At six in the morning, the weather is beautiful, too beautiful, inevitably beautiful... Then, I assure you, one feels afraid. It is appalling to have a whole day which starts with a blazing sun which does not change until it sets."
In *Tahiti II* that ambivalence is present in the juxtaposition of two visual clashes: day and night. The corresponding effects of light are conveyed by the attribution of a color code to the different elements of the landscape. The daytime effects are provided by the blue of the sea, the green of the foliage, and the absence of color in the boat, which expresses the excessiveness of the sunlight, that "thief of color", soon to make regular appearances in advertising films.
The nighttime effects are

Tahiti II, 1936
Gouache on canvas, 238 x 185 cm
Musée Matisse, Le Cateau-Cambrésis

rendered by dark colors distributed at the double border of the sea (the horizon and the shore); the red shade of the mountains, the clouds, and the balcony; the wine-sediment-brown shadow of the sky and the shoreline: "Before the flaming sunset, the sky is the color of honey. Then it turns blue with an infinite sweetness."

This non-realistic treatment of shades gives the impression that *Tahiti II* is the negative of a color photograph. Seventy-five years after Monet's *Impression, Sunrise*, Matisse offers a new vision of landscape. The overall tonality of the painting and the pure lines of the boat recall Mallarmé's lines, "His eye, on the horizon swamped in light,/Sees golden galleons, beautiful as swans," in the poem *Les Fenêtres* (The Windows), for which Matisse did an etching.

Tahiti II is the second version, in gouache (the first *Window in Tahiti* was in oil), of a commission which Matisse did for a cartoon for a tapestry. Here the perspective is reduced to the lines of the boat. All the other motifs are two-dimensional, the colors are applied in blotches, and the curtain, blue like the sea, is hinted at by the effect of transparence, though it keeps its consistency at the level of the sky and the balustrade, a simple theatrical backdrop without relief. Where the frangipani flowers on the frame are not outlined in black, they give the airy feeling of a sea bird. The importance given back to pure colors and the simplification of the outlines enclosing them prefigure the technique of the gouache cutouts.

LARGE INTERIOR IN RED, 1948
Oil on canvas, 146 x 97 cm
*Musée national d'Art moderne,
Paris*

LARGE INTERIOR IN RED

Large Interior in Red is
one of Matisse's last easel
paintings and a summary
of his formal and plastic
investigations of the
previous decade. The
canvas was hung for
the first time in 1949
at the Musée d'Art
Moderne in Paris, which
bought it the
following year.
Red is the dominant
decorative color of
Matisse's large interiors:
The Dinner Table (1908),
The Red Studio (1911).
It is also the color of the
mythical and symbolical
figures in his work, human
(*Dance* 1910, *Music*,
1911) or animal (the
goldfish). Here red is used
both as a decorative
background and a unifying
element for the different
parts of the picture.
Large Interior in Red is
constructed according to
two types of organization
of space.
Vertical organization first,
at the level of the line
perpendicular to the
armchair which marks out
two parts differentiated by
their artistic treatment.
On the left a Chinese ink

representing *Interior with Window and Palm* (1948); identical treatment in black and white of the round table and importance of the line and the empty spaces around the forms; the colors of the flowers themselves lack luster. The handling recalls the evanescent poetry of *Inhabited Silence of Houses* (1947); the objects have no depth and the style is essentially graphic. On the right, primacy of color in the picture hanging on the wall, *Pineapple* (1948), as well as in the composition of the bouquets of flowers, done with dabs of pure juxtaposed colors, revealing a neo-Fauvism in Matisse's work. The obliques of the chair and table create a trǎnsverse perspective movement, reinforced by the position of the animal skins on the floor. And horizontal organization of space; the upper half of the picture is the works within a work, the lower half "reality." In a very Platonic manner,

Large Interior in Red is thus composed of a world above made of memories and reminiscences of the universe of Oceania, characterized here by the exotic plants (palms and pineapples) – the table itself reproduces a miniature lagoon in its colors – and a world below, made of representation, where human presence makes itself felt through the multiplicity of bouquets of flowers on the tables. The picture thus functions as a play of mirrors between memory interiors and material interiors. The unity of the two universes is signified by the balance of the two plastic styles finally achieved by Matisse: line and color. Rather than a neo-Fauvist picture, *Large Interior in Red* is an example of Baroque figuration, also marked by a clash of styles between furniture from different periods: Louis XV table, rustic chair, nineteen-forties wrought iron garden table.

BLUE NUDE III, 1952
Gouache on paper cutout,
112 x 73.5 cm
*Musée national d'Art moderne,
Paris*

BLUE NUDE III

Representation of the human body in the work of Matisse reaches its highest degree of abstraction in the large gouaches done between 1952 and 1954. The series of the four *Blue Nudes* to which *Blue Nude III* belongs is also the end of a long march towards abstraction which Matisse had undertaken in his drawings as well as his paintings.

Monochrome is latent in his work; it imposes itself first of all within the slabs, then in the decorative backgrounds, but without ever reducing the whole work to it.

In his drawings Matisse invented a new plastic language which substitutes signs for real forms. Just as Delacroix ended the movement of the line of an arm with a "claw" and not a hand, Matisse treats the lines of the limbs of a body like signs prolonging their curves, like "arrows."

From drawing, he also learned how to give a void – white – a presence equal to that of black.

In the thirties, his drawing, purged of all modelling, hatching, or streaking, is just lines and whites. The alliance of monochrome and abstract drawing for the representation of a nude was first tried by Matisse in the mural painting *Dance* for Merion. From 1945 he tried to give "the idea of immensity in a limited space." That was to be the technique of the paper cutouts which enabled him to reach this perfection. Matisse made his first cutouts on sheets of inked printing paper; dissatisfied with the result, he turned to paper colored with gouache, which he cut up with scissors; those were the figures of the air (*Icarus, The Clown*) done after 1943 for *Jazz*.

Later Matisse modified his technique; instead of cutting, which produced angular motifs, he carved on the sheet through the matter-color, pushing the edge of the blade forward in a continuous movement. The *Blue Nudes* therefore have a more fluid form.

The drawing itself is constituted by the space separating the colored pieces of the jigsaw puzzle, which also gives the background a function, to constitute the form.

The set of *Blue Nudes* expresses the kinetic decomposition of a single movement of a female body, but each *Nude* is in itself a recomposition of fragments or "partial objects," signifiers of a purely visual desire.

Matisse's *Blue Nudes* are not the trace of a material body as Yves Klein's were to be, but a material imprint of beings emerging from his memories of Oceania, like the mermaids or flying fish.

The *Blue Nudes* are Matisse's "Tahitian Women".

MATISSE

THE COMPLETE WORKS

WORKS

1 • Still Life with Books, 1890
Oil on canvas, 38 x 46 cm
Private Collection

2 • Still Life with Earthenware Pot, 1892
Oil on canvas, 38 x 47 cm
Private Collection

3 • A Pyramid of Fruits, 1893
Oil on canvas, 106 x 86 cm
Private Collection

4 • The Atelier of Gustave Moreau, 1894-1895
Oil on canvas, 65 x 81 cm
Private Collection

5 • Woman Reading, 1895
Oil on wooden panel, 61.5 x 48 cm
Musée national d'Art moderne, Paris

6 • Interior with a Top Hat, 1896
Oil on canvas, 80 x 95 cm
Private Collection

7 • Great Gray Lagoon, 1896
Oil on canvas, 87 x 147 cm
Private Collection

8 • Woman Herding Pigs, 1896
Oil on canvas, 65 x 81 cm

9 • Seascape at Goulphar, 1896
Oil on canvas, 46 x 81 cm
Private Collection

10 • Little Breton Girl, 1896
Oil on panel, 54 x 40 cm
Private Collection

11 • The Bretonne Maid, 1896
Oil on canvas, 90 x 75 cm
Private Collection

12 • Rocks at Belle-Île, 1897
Oil on canvas, 73 x 60 cm
Hahn Gallery Collection, New York

13 • The Dinner Table, 1897
Oil on canvas, 100 x 131 cm
Private Collection

14 • Corsican Landscape, 1898-1899
Oil on canvas, 38 x 46 cm
Musée de l'Annonciade, Saint-Tropez

15 • First Orange Still Life, 1899
Oil on canvas, 56 x 73 cm
Musée national d'Art moderne, Paris

16 • Male Model, 1900
Oil on canvas, 99.3 x 72.7 cm
The Museum of Modern Art, New York

1

2

3

4

5

6

7

8

9

10

11

12

13

14

15

16

17

18

19   20

21   22   23

24   25   26

27   28   29

30   31   32

17 • Model with Rose Slippers, 1900
Oil on canvas, 73 x 60 cm
Jan Krugier Gallery, Geneva

**18 • Still Life with
a Chocolate Pot, 1900**
Oil on canvas, 73 x 59.5 cm
*Formerly Alex Maguy Collection,
Paris*

19 • The Serf, 1900-1903
Bronze, 92.3 x 34.5 x 33 cm
Musée Matisse, Le Cateau-Cambrésis

20 • Portrait of Bevilacqua, 1901
Oil on canvas, 35 x 27 cm
Formerly Marquet Collection, Paris

21 • Along the Edge of the Road, 1901
Oil on canvas, 21.5 x 36 cm
Private Collection

**22 • Madame Matisse in
a Japanese Dress, 1901**
Oil on canvas, 116 x 80 cm
Private Collection

23 • Madeleine I, 1901
Bronze, 59.7 x 19.7 x 22.9 cm
Private Collection

24 • Studio Under the Eaves, 1903
Oil on canvas, 55.2 x 46 cm
Fitzwilliam Museum, Cambridge

25 • The River-Walk, 1903
Oil on canvas, 50 x 39 cm

**26 • Still Life with Red Checked
Cloth, 1903**
Oil on canvas, 52 x 53 cm

27 • Nude with a White Towel, 1903
Oil on canvas, 81 x 59 cm
The Phillips Collection, Washington

28 • Guitarist, 1903
Oil on canvas, 54 x 38 cm
The Colin Collection, New York

**29 • Bouquet on a Bamboo
Table, 1903**
Oil on canvas, 54.6 x 45 cm
Private Collection

30 • Luxe, calme et volupté, 1904
Oil on canvas, 32.2 x 40.5 cm
*Mrs. John Hay Whitney Collection,
New York*

**31 • The Place des Lices
(Saint-Tropez), 1904**
Oil on canvas, 51 x 56 cm
*Statens Museum for Kunst,
Copenhagen*

**32 • The Terrace at Signac
(Saint-Tropez), 1904**
Oil on canvas, 71 x 56 cm
*Isabella Stewart Gardner Museum,
Boston*

WORKS

33 • Still Life with a Purro I, 1904
Oil on canvas, 59 x 72.4 cm
The Phillips Collection, Washington

**34 • Le Goûter or The Gulf
of Saint-Tropez, 1904**
Oil on canvas, 65 x 50.5 cm
*Kunstsammlung Nordrhein-Westfalen,
Düsseldorf*

35 • View of Saint-Tropez, 1904
Oil on canvas, 35 x 48 cm
*Musée de Bagnols-sur-Cèze
(stolen in 1972)*

36 • St. Anne's Chapel, 1904
Oil on canvas, 60 x 73 cm
Private Collection

37 • Breton Landscape, 1904
Oil on canvas, 46 x 55 cm
Museu de Arte, São Paulo

38 • Luxe, calme et volupté, 1904
Oil on canvas, 98.5 x 118.5 cm
*Musée d'Orsay (on loan from the
Musée national d'Art moderne), Paris*

39 • Still Life with a Purro II, 1904 (?)
Oil on canvas, 27.3 x 35.6 cm
*Mrs. John Hay Whitney Collection,
New York*

40 • Notre-Dame, 1904-1905
Oil on canvas, 45 x 55 cm
Moderna Museet, Stockholm

41 • Notre-Dame, 1904-1905 (?)
Oil on canvas, 22.4 x 32.5 cm
Private Collection

42 • Parrot Tulips I, 1905
Oil on canvas, 46 x 55 cm

43 • Parrot Tulips II, 1905
Oil on panel, 46 x 55 cm
Private Collection

**44 • Still Life, Dishes on the Table
(Still Life with Cameo), 1904-1905 (?)**
Oil on canvas, 73 x 92 cm
*The Hermitage Museum, St.
Petersburg*

**45 • Landscape at Collioure
(The Belfry), 1905**
Oil on canvas, 38 x 46 cm
Steichen Collection, New York

**46 • Rue du Soleil
(Street at Collioure), 1905**
Oil on canvas, 46 x 55 cm
Private Collection

47 • Olive Trees at Collioure, 1905
Oil on canvas, 46 x 54 cm
Private Collection

48 • Trees in Collioure, 1905
Oil on canvas
Robert Lehman Foundation, New York

33

34

35

36

37

38

39

40

41

42

43

44

45

46

47

48

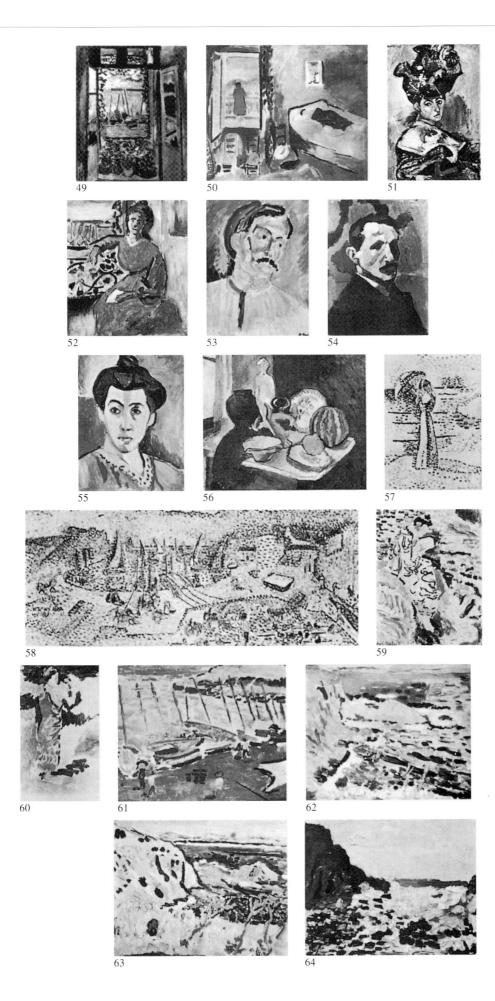

49   50   51

52   53   54

55   56   57

58   59

60   61   62

63   64

49 • Open Window in Collioure, 1905
Oil on canvas, 55.2 x 46 cm
Mrs. John Hay Whitney Collection,
New York

50 • Interior at Collioure
(The Siesta), 1905
Oil on canvas, 60 x 73 cm
Private Collection

51 • Woman in a Hat, 1905
Oil on canvas, 80.6 x 59.7 cm
Museum of Modern Art, San Francisco

52 • Woman at the Window, 1905
Oil on canvas, 31.8 x 29.8 cm
Private Collection

53 • André Derain, 1905
Oil on canvas, 39.4 x 28.9 cm
The Tate Gallery, London

54 • Portrait of Albert Marquet, 1905
Oil on wood, 41.5 x 31 cm
Nasjonalgalleriet, Oslo

55 • Portrait of Madame Matisse
(The Green Line), 1905
Oil on canvas, 40.5 x 32.5 cm
Statens Museum for Kunst,
Copenhagen

56 • Still Life with Melon, 1905
Oil on canvas, 66 x 81 cm
The Barnes Foundation, Merion

57 • Young Girl with Parasol, 1905
Oil on canvas, 46 x 35 cm
Musée Matisse, Nice

58 • The Port of Abaill, 1905
Oil on canvas, 60 x 148 cm
Private Collection

59 • La Japonaise: Woman Beside
the Water, 1905
Oil and crayon on canvas,
35.2 x 28.2 cm
The Museum of Modern Art, New York

60 • Figure, Standing, 1905
Oil on wood, 31 x 19 cm
The Barnes Foundation, Merion

61 • The Red Beach, 1905
Oil on canvas, 33 x 41 cm
Fridart Foundation

62 • Seascape: La Moulade, 1905
Oil on canvas, 24.2 x 32.3 cm
Private Collection

63 • Seascape: La Moulade, 1905
Oil on cardboard mounted on panel,
26.1 x 33.7 cm
Museum of Modern Art, San Francisco

64 • Seascape: Beside the Sea, 1905
Oil on cardboard mounted on panel,
24.5 x 32.4 cm
Museum of Modern Art, San Francisco

WORKS

65 • Landscape at Collioure, 1905
Oil on canvas, 46 x 55 cm
Statens Museum for Kunst,
Copenhagen

66 • Le Canal du Midi, 1905 (?)
Oil on canvas, 24 x 36.5 cm

67 • Landscape at Collioure,
1905-1906
Oil on canvas, 38 x 45 cm
The Barnes Foundation, Merion

68 • The Idol, 1905-1906
Oil on canvas, 73 x 60 cm
Private Collection

69 • Interior with a Young Girl
(Girl Reading), 1905-1906
Oil on canvas, 72.7 x 59.4 cm
Private Collection

70 • The Roofs of Collioure,
1905-1906 (?)
Oil on canvas, 59.5 x 73 cm
The Hermitage Museum,
St. Petersburg

71 • Cucumbers, 1905 or 1906 (?)
Oil on canvas, 38 x 46 cm
Gelman Collection, Mexico

72 • Pastorale, 1906
Oil on canvas, 45.7 x 55.2 cm
Musée d'Art moderne de
la Ville de Paris

73 • Nude in a Wood, 1906
Oil on canvas, 40.6 x 32.4 cm
The Brooklyn Museum, New York

74 • La Joie de vivre, 1906
Oil on canvas, 174 x 238.1 cm
The Barnes Foundation, Merion

75 • Sketch for La Joie
de vivre, 1906
Oil on canvas, 40.6 x 54.6 cm
Museum of Modern Art, San Francisco

76 • Sketch for La Joie
de vivre, 1906
Oil on panel, 12 x 19 cm
The Barnes Foundation, Merion

77 • Landscape in Algeria, 1906
Oil on canvas, 34 x 41 cm
Statens Museum for Kunst,
Copenhagen

78 • Pont Saint-Michel, 1906
Oil on canvas, 64.8 x 80.6 cm
Burden Collection, New York

79 • Gypsy (Woman's Bust), 1906
Oil on canvas, 55 x 46 cm
Musée de l'Annonciade, Saint-Tropez

80 • Still Life with a Red Rug, 1906
Oil on canvas, 89 x 116.5 cm
Musée de Grenoble, Grenoble

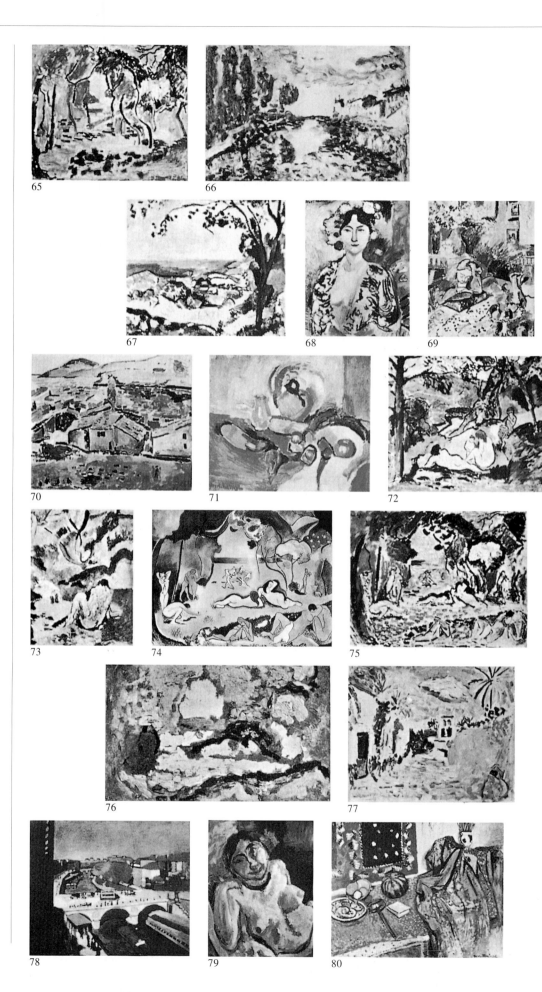

81 • Provençal Ceramics, 1906
Oil on canvas, 54 x 45 cm
The Museum of Art, Baltimore

**82 • Still Life with a
Plaster Figure, 1906**
Oil on canvas, 54 x 45 cm
*Yale University Art Gallery,
New Haven (Connecticut)*

83 • Sails, 1906
Oil on canvas, 25 x 59 cm
Private Collection

84 • Vase of Flowers, 1906
Oil on canvas, 19 x 24.5 cm
The Art Institute, Chicago

85 • Seated Nude, 1906
Oil on panel, 33 x 41 cm
The Barnes Foundation, Merion

**86 • Reclining Nude
(Nude in the Grass), 1906**
Oil on canvas, 28 x 38 cm
Private Collection

87 • Nude Seated in Landscape, 1906
Oil on canvas, 40 x 32 cm
Findlay Galleries, Chicago

88 • Marguerite Reading, 1906
Oil on canvas, 64 x 80 cm
Musée de Grenoble

89 • Marguerite, 1906
Oil on panel, 31.8 x 24.1 cm
*Nathan and Marion Smooke
Collection*

90 • Nude, Near Screen, 1906
Oil on canvas, 33 x 19 cm
Ardrey Collection, Norman

91 • Self-Portrait, 1906
Oil on canvas, 55 x 46 cm
*Statens Museum for Kunst,
Copenhagen*

92 • Woman on the Terrace, 1906
Oil on canvas, 65 x 80.5 cm
*The Hermitage Museum,
St. Petersburg*

**93 • Dishes and Fruits on a Red
and Black Cloth, 1906**
Oil on canvas, 61 x 73 cm
*The Hermitage Museum,
St. Petersburg*

94 • La Vie (Torso with Head), 1906
Bronze, 23.2 x 10.2 x 7.6 cm
Private Collection

**95 • Still Life with a Geranium,
1906-1907**
Oil on canvas, 97.9 x 80.2 cm
The Art Institute, Chicago

96 • Pink Onions, 1906-1907 (?)
Oil on canvas, 46 x 55 cm
*Statens Museum for Kunst,
Copenhagen*

WORKS

97 • Marguerite, 1906-1907
Oil on canvas, 56 x 46 cm
Private Collection

98 • Marguerite, 1906-1907
Oil on canvas, 65 x 54 cm
Musée Picasso, Paris

99 • Nude in a Tube, 1906-1907
Oil on canvas, 55 x 66 cm
Private Collection

100 • Standing Nude, 1906-1907
Oil on canvas, 92 x 65 cm
The Tate Gallery, London

**101 • The Young Sailor I,
1906-1907 (?)**
Oil on canvas, 100 x 78.5 cm
Private Collection

102 • Young Sailor II, 1906-1907 (?)
Oil on canvas, 100 x 81 cm
Gelman Collection, Mexico

103 • Vase of Flowers, 1907
Oil on canvas
Aubry Collection, Paris

104 • Rose in a Vase, 1907
Oil on canvas, 40 x 32 cm
Private Collection

105 • Blue Still Life, 1907
Oil on canvas, 89 x 117 cm
The Barnes Foundation, Merion

106 • The Hairdressing, 1907
Oil on canvas, 116 x 89 cm
Staatsgalerie, Stuttgart

**107 • Blue Nude
(Souvenir of Biskra), 1907**
Oil on canvas, 92.1 x 140.4 cm
The Museum of Art, Baltimore

108 • Reclining Nude I, 1906-1907
Bronze, 35 x 50 x 27.5 cm
Musée national d'Art moderne, Paris

109 • Luxe I, 1907
Oil on canvas, 210 x 138 cm
Musée national d'Art moderne, Paris

110 • Two Women, 1907
Bronze, 49.5 x 28 x 20 cm
Musée national d'Art moderne, Paris

111 • Luxe II, 1907-1908
Oil on canvas, 209.5 x 138 cm
*Statens Museum for Kunst,
Copenhagen*

112 • The Madras Turban, 1907
Oil on panel, 33 x 41 cm
The Barnes Foundation, Merion

97

98

99

100

101

102

103

104

105

106

107

108

109

110

111

112

MATISSE

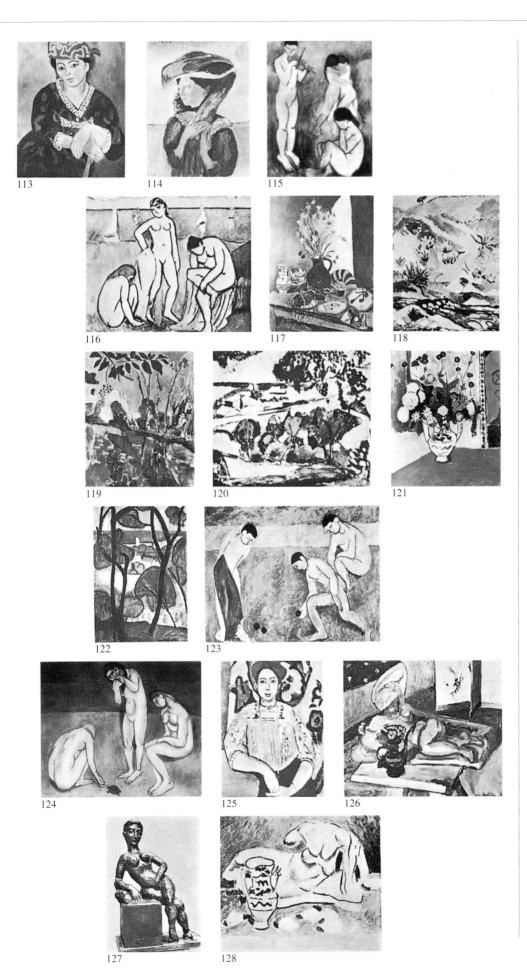

**113 • Madame Matisse
in Madras, 1907**
Oil on canvas, 99 x 81 cm
The Barnes Foundation, Merion

114 • Margot, 1907
Oil on canvas, 81 x 65 cm
Kunsthaus, Zurich

115 • Music (oil sketch), 1907
Oil on canvas, 73.4 x 60.8 cm
The Museum of Modern Art, New York

116 • Bathers, 1907
Oil on canvas, 59 x 73 cm
The Institute of Arts, Minneapolis

117 • Still Life with Asphodels, 1907
Oil on canvas, 114 x 87 cm
Museum Folkwang, Essen

118 • Brook with Aloes, 1907
Oil on canvas, 73 x 60 cm
The Menil Collection, Houston

119 • River Bank, 1907
Oil on canvas, 73 x 60.5 cm
Kunstmuseum, Basel

120 • Paysage, Collioure, 1907
Oil on canvas
Private Collection

**121 • Bouquet. Vase with
Two Handles, 1907**
Oil on canvas, 74 x 61 cm
*The Hermitage Museum,
St. Petersburg*

122 • View of Collioure, 1907-1908 (?)
Oil on canvas, 92 x 65.5 cm
Gelman Collection, Mexico

123 • Game of Bowls, 1908
Oil on canvas, 113.5 x 145 cm
*The Hermitage Museum,
St. Petersburg*

124 • Bathers with Turtle, 1908
Oil on canvas, 179.1 x 220.3 cm
The Art Museum, St. Louis

125 • Portrait of Greta Moll, 1908
Oil on canvas, 93 x 73 cm
The National Gallery, London

**126 • Sculpture and Persian
Vase, 1908**
Oil on canvas, 60.5 x 73.5 cm
Nasjonalgalleriet, Oslo

127 • Decorative Figure, 1908
Bronze, 72.1 x 51.4 x 31.1 cm
*Hirshhorn Museum and Sculpture
Garden, Washington*

128 • Still Life with Greek Torso, 1908
Oil on canvas, 63 x 76 cm

WORKS

129 • Still Life with Blue Tablecloth, 1908-1909
Oil on canvas, 88 x 118 cm
The Hermitage Museum, St. Petersburg

130 • Still Life in Venice Red (Statuette and Vase on an Oriental Rug), 1908
Oil on canvas, 80 x 105 cm
Pushkin Museum, Moscow

131 • Vase of Flowers, 1908
Oil on canvas
The Barnes Foundation, Merion

132 • The Girl with Green Eyes, 1908
Oil on canvas, 66 x 50.8 cm
Museum of Modern Art, San Francisco

133 • Nude, Black and Gold, 1908
Oil on canvas, 100 x 65 cm
The Hermitage Museum, St. Petersburg

134 • Nymph and Satyr, 1908
Oil on canvas, 89 x 117 cm
The Hermitage Museum, St. Petersburg

135 • Nude, Black and Gold, 1908
Oil on canvas, 100 x 65 cm
The Hermitage Museum, St. Petersburg

136 • Seated Nude, 1908
Oil on canvas, 80.5 x 52 cm
The Hermitage Museum, St. Petersburg

137 • The Dessert: A Harmony in Red, 1908
Oil on canvas, 180 x 220 cm
The Hermitage Museum, St. Petersburg

138 • The Back I, 1908-1909
Bronze, 190 x 116 x 13 cm
Musée national d'Art moderne, Paris

139 • Child with a Butterfly Net (Alan Stein), 1909
Oil on canvas, 175 x 112.5 cm
The Institute of Arts, Minneapolis

140 • Spanish Woman with a Tambourine, 1909
Oil on canvas, 92 x 73 cm
Pushkin Museum, Moscow

141 • Dance, 1909
Oil on canvas, 259.7 x 390.1 cm
The Museum of Modern Art, New York

142 • Algerian Woman, 1909
Oil on canvas, 81 x 65 cm
Musée national d'Art moderne, Paris

143 • Lady in Green, 1909
Oil on canvas, 65 x 54 cm
The Hermitage Museum, St. Petersburg

144 • Seated Girl, 1909
Oil on canvas, 41.5 x 33.5 cm
Wallraf-Richartz Museum, Cologne

129

130

131

132

133

134

135

136

137

138

139

140

141

142

143

144

145

146

147

149

150

151

151A

152

153

154

155

156

157

158

159

145 • Portrait of Pierre Matisse, 1909
Oil on canvas, 40.6 x 33 cm
Private Collection

**146 • The Forest of
Fontainebleau, 1909**
Oil on canvas, 61 x 74 cm
Sigri Welhaven Collection, Oslo

147 • Pink Nude (Seated Nude), 1909
Oil on canvas, 33 x 40 cm
Musée de Grenoble, Grenoble

148 • Nude in Sunny Landscape, 1909
Oil on canvas, 42 x 33 cm
Jacobs Collection, San Francisco

**149 • Nude on the Shores
of the Sea, 1909**
Oil on canvas, 61 x 117 cm

150 • Bather, 1909
Oil on canvas, 92.7 x 74 cm
The Museum of Modern Art, New York

151 • Fruits and Flowers, 1909
Oil on canvas, 73 x 60 cm
Ordrupgaardsamlingen, Copenhagen

151A • La Serpentine, 1909
Bronze, 56.5 x 28 x 19 cm
The Museum of Modern Art, New York

152 • Still Life with Dance, 1909
Oil on canvas, 89 x 116 cm
*The Hermitage Museum,
St. Petersburg*

153 • Goldfish, 1909-1910
Oil on canvas, 82 x 93 cm
*Statens Museum for Kunst,
Copenhagen*

154 • Dance, 1910
Oil on canvas, 260 x 391 cm
*The Hermitage Museum,
St. Petersburg*

155 • Music, 1910
Oil on canvas, 260 x 389 cm
*The Hermitage Museum,
St. Petersburg*

**156 • Still Life with a Pewter Jug
and Pink Statuette, 1910**
Oil on canvas, 90 x 117 cm
*The Hermitage Museum,
St. Petersburg*

**157 • Still Life with
Geraniums, 1910**
Oil on canvas, 94.5 x 116 cm
*Bayerische
Staatsgemäldesammlungen,
Neue Pinakothek, Munich*

158 • Bronze and Fruits, 1910
Oil on canvas, 90 x 115 cm
Pushkin Museum, Moscow

**159 • Girl with Tulips
(Jeanne Vaderin), 1910**
Oil on canvas, 92 x 73.5 cm
*The Hermitage Museum,
St. Petersburg*

WORKS

160 • Jeannette I, 1910
Bronze, 50 x 22.5 x 26.5 cm
Musée national d'Art moderne, Paris

161 • Jeannette II, 1910
Bronze, 33 x 25.4 x 27.9 cm
Private Collection

**162 • Marguerite with Black Cat
(Girl with Cat), 1910**
Oil on canvas, 94 x 64 cm
Private Collection

163 • Seville Still Life, 1910-1911
Oil on canvas, 90 x 117 cm
*The Hermitage Museum,
St. Petersburg*

164 • Spanish Still Life, 1910-1911
Oil on canvas, 89 x 116 cm
*The Hermitage Museum,
St. Petersburg*

165 • The Manila Shawl, 1911
Oil on canvas, 118 x 75.5 cm
Rudolf Staechelin Foundation, Basel

166 • Jeannette III, 1910-1911
Bronze, 60.3 x 26 x 28 cm
Private Collection

167 • Jeannette IV, 1910-1911
Bronze, 61.5 x 22 x 28 cm
Musée national d'Art moderne, Paris

168 • The Painter's Family, 1911
Oil on canvas, 143 x 194 cm
*The Hermitage Museum,
St. Petersburg*

169 • Portrait of Olga Merson, 1911
Oil on canvas, 100.1 x 80.6 cm
The Museum of Fine Arts, Houston

170 • Seated Nude (Olga), 1911
Bronze, 42.5 x 24.5 x 33 cm
Private Collection

171 • The Pink Studio, 1911
Oil on canvas, 180 x 221 cm
Pushkin Museum, Moscow

172 • View of Collioure, 1911
Oil on canvas, 90.2 x 118.1 cm
*Mr. and Mrs. Donald B. Marron
Collection, New York*

**173 • View of Collioure
and the Sea, 1911**
Oil on canvas, 61 x 49.6 cm
The Museum of Modern Art, New York

174 • Interior with Aubergines, 1911
Distemper on canvas, 212 x 246 cm
Musée de Grenoble, Grenoble

175 • The Conversation, 1909-1912
Oil on canvas, 177 x 217 cm
*The Hermitage Museum,
St. Petersburg*

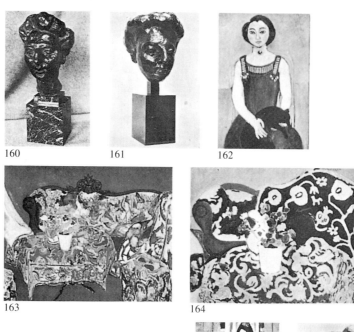
160   161   162

163

164

165   166   167

168

169   170

171   172   173

174   175

176

177

178

179

180

181

182

183

184

185

186

187

188

189

190

191

176 • Flowers and Ceramic Plate, 1911
Oil on canvas, 93.5 x 82.5 cm
Städelsches Kunstinstitut und
Städische Galerie, Frankfurt

177 • The Red Studio, 1911
Oil on canvas, 181 x 219.1 cm
The Museum of Modern Art, New York

178 • Joaquina, 1911
Oil on canvas, 55 x 38.5 cm
Národní Galeri, Prague

179 • The Seine at Paris, c. 1911
Oil on canvas, 26.5 x 35 cm

180 • Purple Cyclamen, 1911-1912
Oil on canvas, 73 x 60 cm
Private Collection

181 • Periwinkles
(Moroccan Gardens), 1912
Oil, pencil and charcoal on canvas,
116.8 x 82.5 cm
The Museum of Modern Art, New York

182 • The Palm Tree (March
Morning Near Tangiers), 1912
Oil on canvas, 116 x 81 cm
National Gallery of Art, Washington

183 • Basket of Oranges, 1912
Oil on canvas, 94 x 83 cm
Musée Picasso, Paris

184 • Acanthus (Forest Floor or
Moroccan Landscape), 1912
Oil on canvas, 116 x 81 cm
Moderna Museet, Stockholm

185 • Goldfish, 1912
Oil on canvas, 147 x 98 cm
Pushkin Museum, Moscow

186 • Nasturtiums
with Dance I, 1912
Oil on canvas, 191.8 x 115.3 cm
The Metropolitan Museum of Art, New
York

187 • Nasturtiums with
Dance II, 1912
Oil on canvas, 190.5 x 114 cm
Pushkin Museum, Moscow

188 • Goldfish and Sculpture, 1912
Oil on canvas, 116.2 x 100.5 cm
The Museum of Modern Art, New York

189 • Interior with Red Fish, 1912
Oil on canvas, 117 x 102 cm
The Barnes Foundation, Merion

190 • The Geraniums Pot, 1912
Oil on canvas, 41.3 x 33.3 cm
National Gallery of Art, Washington

191 • Still Life with Plaster Bust, 1912
Oil on canvas, 99 x 79 cm
The Barnes Foundation, Merion

WORKS

**192 • Bunch of Irises on
the Veranda, 1912-1913**
Oil on canvas, 146 x 97 cm
*The Hermitage Museum,
St. Petersburg*

193 • Amido the Moroccan, 1912
Oil on canvas, 146 x 62 cm
*The Hermitage Museum,
St. Petersburg*

194 • The Moroccan Woman, 1912
Oil on canvas, 36 x 28 cm
Musée de Grenoble, Grenoble

195 • Zorah Standing, 1912
Oil on canvas, 146 x 61 cm
The Hermitage Museum, St. Petersburg

196 • The Yellow Dress (Zorah), 1912
Oil on canvas, 89 x 63.5 cm
*Cowles Collection, Lake Forest
(Illinois)*

**197 • Landscape Seen from
a Window, 1912**
Oil on canvas, 115 x 80 cm
Pushkin Museum, Moscow

**198 • View of the Bay
of Tangiers, 1912**
Oil on canvas, 45 x 55 cm
Musée de Grenoble, Grenoble

199 • The Standing Rifain, 1912
Oil on canvas, 145 x 96.5 cm
*The Hermitage Museum,
St. Petersburg*

200 • Vase of Irises, 1912
Oil on canvas, 118 x 100 cm
*The Hermitage Museum,
St. Petersburg*

**201 • The Gate to the Casbah,
1912-1913**
Oil on canvas, 116 x 80 cm
*The Hermitage Museum,
St. Petersburg*

**202 • Zorah on the Terrace,
1912-1913**
Oil on canvas, 116 x 80 cm
Pushkin Museum, Moscow

203 • The Blue Window, 1913
Oil on canvas, 130.8 x 90.5 cm
The Museum of Modern Art, New York

**204 • Portrait of
Madame Matisse, 1913**
Oil on canvas, 145 x 97 cm
*The Hermitage Museum,
St. Petersburg*

**205 • Calla Lilies, Irises,
and Mimosas, 1913**
Oil on canvas, 145.5 x 98 cm
Pushkin Museum, Moscow

206 • Rifain Seated, 1913
Oil on canvas, 200 x 159 cm
The Barnes Foundation, Merion

207 • Mulatto Woman, 1913
Oil on canvas, 146 x 61 cm
Müller Collection, Soluthern

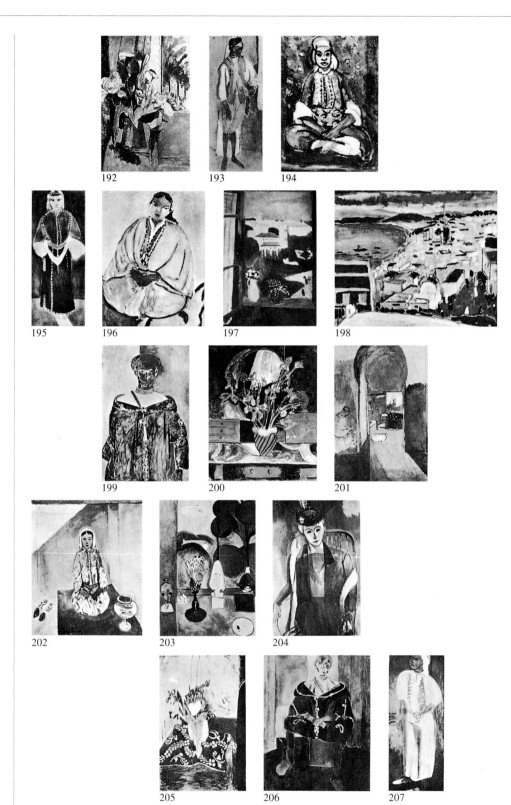

192   193   194

195   196   197   198

199   200   201

202   203   204

205   206   207

208

209

210

211

212

213

214

215

216

217

218

219

220

221

222

223

208 • The Arab Café, 1913
Oil on canvas, 176 x 210 cm
*The Hermitage Museum, St.
Petersburg*

**209 • Tangiers Landscape from
Open Window, 1913**
Oil on canvas, 145 x 94 cm

210 • The Back II, 1913
Bronze, 188 x 116 x 14 cm
Musée national d'Art moderne, Paris

211 • Woman and Stool, 1913-1914 (?)
Oil on canvas, 147 x 95.5 cm
The Museum of Modern Art, New York

212 • Branch of Lilacs, 1914
Oil on canvas, 146 x 97.2 cm
Private Collection

**213 • Mademoiselle Yvonne
Landsberg, 1914**
Oil on canvas, 147.3 x 97.5 cm
The Museum of Art, Philadelphia

214 • Interior, Goldfish Bowl, 1914
Oil on canvas, 147 x 97 cm
Musée national d'Art moderne, Paris

**215 • French Window
at Collioure, 1914**
Oil on canvas, 118.5 x 89 cm
Musée national d'Art moderne, Paris

216 • White and Pink Head, 1914
Oil on canvas, 75 x 47 cm
Musée national d'Art moderne, Paris

217 • View of Notre-Dame, 1914
Oil on canvas, 145 x 98 cm
Art Museum, Soluthern

218 • View of Notre-Dame, 1914
Oil on canvas, 147.3 x 94.3 cm
The Museum of Modern Art, New York

**219 • Still Life with Lemons which
Corresponds in Form to a Drawing
of a Black Vase on the Wall, 1914**
Oil on canvas, 71 x 56 cm
*Museum of Art, Rhode Island School
of Design, Providence*

220 • Goldfish and Palette, 1914-1915
Oil on canvas, 146.5 x 112.4 cm
The Museum of Modern Art, New York

221 • The Yellow Curtain, 1915
Oil on canvas, 146 x 97 cm
Stephen Hahn Collection, New York

222 • Branch of Ivy, 1915
Oil on canvas, 60 x 50 cm
Zumsteg Collection, Zurich

223 • Still Life with Fruits, 1915
Oil on canvas, 46 x 74 cm
Rockefeller Collection, New York

WORKS

224 • Woman with Straw Hat, 1915
Oil on canvas
Ishibashi Collection, Tokyo

**225 • Still Life after Jan Davidsz.
De Heem's La Desserte, 1915**
Oil on canvas, 180.9 x 220.8 cm
The Museum of Modern Art, New York

226 • Still Life with Calabash, 1915
Oil on canvas
*Museum of Art, Rhode Island School
of Design, Providence (Rhode Island)*

227 • Head of Marguerite, 1915 (?)
Bronze, 32 cm
Private Collection

228 • The Moroccans, 1915-1916
Oil on canvas, 181.3 x 279.4 cm
The Museum of Modern Art, New York

**229 • Still Life with Fruit and
Flowers, 1915-1916**
Oil on canvas, 36 x 27.5 cm

230 • The Colocynths, 1915-1916
Oil on canvas, 65.1 x 80.9 cm
The Museum of Modern Art, New York

231 • The Italian Woman, 1916
Oil on canvas, 116.7 x 89.5 cm
*Solomon R. Guggenheim Museum,
New York*

232 • Cup of Oranges, 1916
Oil on canvas, 54 x 65 cm
Private Collection

233 • The Window, 1916
Oil on canvas, 146 x 116.8 cm
The Institute of Arts, Detroit

234 • The Three Sisters, 1916
Oil on canvas, 92 x 73 cm
Musée de l'Orangerie, Paris

235 • Bathers by a River, 1916
Oil on canvas, 261.8 x 391.4 cm
The Art Institute, Chicago

236 • The Piano Lesson, 1916
Oil on canvas, 245.1 x 212.7 cm
The Museum of Modern Art, New York

237 • The Rose Marble Table, 1916
Oil on canvas, 146 x 97 cm
The Museum of Modern Art, New York

238 • The Back III, 1916
Bronze, 190 x 114 x 16 cm
Musée national d'Art moderne, Paris

239 • Jeannette V, 1916
Bronze, 56 x 19 x 27 cm
Private Collection

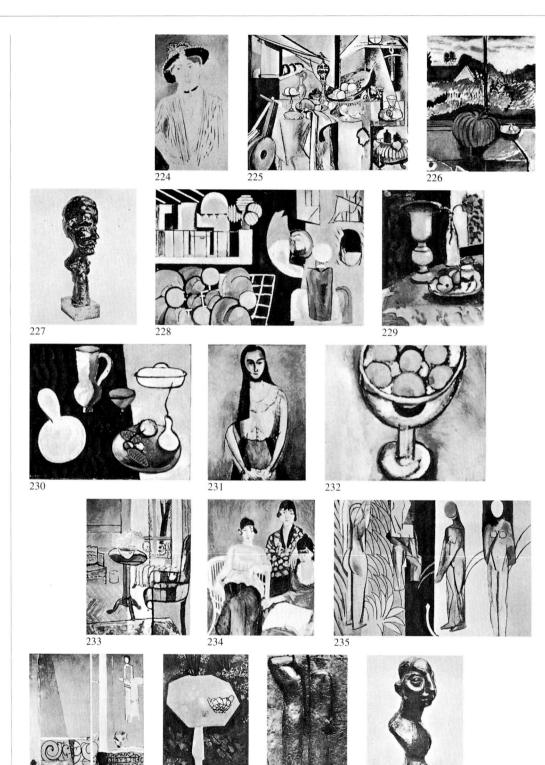

224   225   226

227   228   229

230   231   232

233   234   235

236   237   238   239

240

241

242

243

244

245

246

247

248

249

250

251

252

253

254

255

240 • Apples, 1916
Oil on canvas, 116.9 x 88.9 cm
The Art Institute, Chicago

241 • Woman with White Neck, 1916
Oil on canvas, 22 x 15.5 cm

242 • Portrait of Sarah Stein, 1916
Oil on canvas, 72.4 x 56.5 cm
Museum of Modern Art, San Francisco

243 • Portrait of Michael Stein, 1916
Oil on canvas, 67.3 x 50.4 cm
Museum of Modern Art, San Francisco

244 • Auguste Pellerin I, 1916
Oil on canvas, 92.3 x 78.5 cm
Private Collection

245 • Portrait of Greta Prozor, 1916
Oil on canvas, 146 x 96 cm
Musée national d'Art moderne, Paris

**246 • Woman Seated
in an Armchair, 1916**
Oil on canvas, 41 x 33 cm

247 • Bowl of Apples on a Table, 1916
Oil on canvas, 114.9 x 89.5 cm
*The Chrysler Museum, Norfolk
(Virginia)*

248 • Still Life with Lemon, 1916
Oil on canvas, 26 x 33.5 cm
The Barnes Foundation, Merion

**249 • Lorette, with
White Turban, 1916**
Oil on canvas, 35 x 26 cm
Cohn Collection, New York

**250 • Woman with Amber
Necklace, 1917**
Oil on canvas, 55.5 x 46.5 cm
Private Collection

**251 • Portrait of Marguerite
a Black Velvet ribbon, 1916**
Oil on panel, 18 x 17 cm
Private Collection

**252 • Woman with Turban
(Lorette), 1916**
Oil on panel, 22.5 x 16 cm

253 • Head of a Girl, 1916
Oil on canvas, 35 x 24 cm

**254 • Fruit Basket with
Nutcrackers, 1916**
Oil on canvas, 61 x 49.5 cm
*Statens Museum for Kunst,
Copenhagen*

255 • Green Dress, 1916
Oil on canvas, 73 x 54.5 cm
The Colin Collection, New York

WORKS

**256 • Woman in a Turban
(Lorette), 1916-1917 (?)**
Oil on canvas, 81.3 x 65.4 cm
The Museum of Art, Baltimore

**257 • The Studio,
Quai Saint-Michel, 1916-1917**
Oil on canvas, 147.9 x 116.8 cm
The Phillips Collection, Washington

258 • Lorette Reclining, 1916-1917
Oil on canvas, 95 x 196 cm
Private Collection

**259 • Lorette in a Green Robe
against a Black Background,
1916-1917**
Oil on canvas, 73 x 55 cm
Gelman Collection, Mexico

**260 • Lorette with White Blouse,
1916-1917**
Oil on canvas, 53.3 x 46 cm
Lewisohn Collection, New York

261 • Oriental Lunch, 1917
Oil on canvas, 100.6 x 65.4 cm
The Institute of Arts, Detroit

**262 • The Painter in His Studio
(The Painter and His model,
or The Studio, Quai Saint-Michel),
1916-1917**
Oil on canvas, 146.5 x 97 cm
Musée national d'Art moderne, Paris

263 • The Pewter Jug, 1916-1917
Oil on canvas, 92.1 x 65.1 cm
The Museum of Art, Baltimore

264 • Road to Clamart, 1916-1917
Oil on canvas, 33.5 x 46.5 cm
Musée national d'Art moderne, Paris

**265 • Auguste Pellerin II,
1916-1917 (?)**
Oil on canvas, 150.2 x 96.2 cm
Musée national d'Art moderne, Paris

266 • Trivaux Pond, 1917
Oil on canvas, 92.7 x 74.3 cm
The Tate Gallery, London

**267 • Female Head with
Coffee Cup, 1917**
Oil on canvas, 66 x 43 cm

268 • Head of a Woman, 1917
Oil on canvas, 56 x 30 cm

269 • Head of a Woman, 1917
Oil on panel, 35 x 27 cm
The Museum of Art, Philadelphia

270 • Seated in a Pink Armchair, 1917
Oil on canvas, 100 x 73 cm
Private Collection

271 • Lorette, 1917
Oil on panel, 61.3 x 49.4 cm
National Gallery of Art, Washington

256

257

258

259

260

261

262

263

264

265

266

267

268

269

270

271

272   273

274   275   276

277   278

279   280   281

282   283

284   285

272 • **Peaches with Pewter Jar, 1917**
Oil on panel, 50 x 40 cm
Private Collection

273 • **Aïcha and Lorette, 1917**
Oil on canvas, 38 x 46 cm
Private Collection

274 • **The Music Lesson, 1917**
Oil on canvas, 245 x 209.5 cm
The Barnes Foundation, Merion

275 • **Interior at Nice, 1917**
Oil on canvas, 63 x 45 cm

276 • **Shaft of Sunlight,
the Woods of Trivaux, 1917**
Oil on canvas, 91 x 74 cm
Private Collection

277 • **The Villacoublay Road, 1917**
Oil on canvas, 38 x 55 cm
The Museum of Fine Arts, Cleveland

278 • **The Blue Villa, 1917**
Oil on canvas, 33 x 41 cm
The Barnes Foundation, Merion

279 • **Eucalyptus at Montalban, 1917**
Oil on canvas, 34 x 47 cm
The Museum of Art, Baltimore

280 • **The Bay of Nice, 1917**
Oil on canvas, 90 x 71 cm
Private Collection

281 • **Girl in Black on
the Balcony, 1917**
Oil on canvas, 41 x 33 cm
The Barnes Foundation, Merion

282 • **Nude Seated, 1917**
Oil on canvas, 40 x 32 cm
Paul Valloton Collection, Lausanne

283 • **Nude Posing, 1917**
Oil on canvas, 41 x 33 cm
The Barnes Foundation, Merion

284 • **Head of a Girl, 1917**
Oil on panel, 35 x 26.5 cm
The Barnes Foundation, Merion

285 • **George Besson I, 1917**
Oil on panel, 14 x 8 cm
Musée Albert André, Bagnols-sur-Cèze

286 • The Three Sisters with the Black Sculpture, 1917
Oil on canvas, 195.5 x 96.8 cm
The Barnes Foundation, Merion

287 • The Three Sisters on a Gray Background, 1917
Oil on canvas, 195.5 x 96.8 cm
The Barnes Foundation, Merion

288 • The Three Sisters at the Pink Marble Table, 1917
Oil on canvas, 193.8 x 95.7 cm
The Barnes Foundation, Merion

289 • The Two Sisters, 1917 (?)
Oil on canvas, 65 x 54 cm
Art Museum, Denver

290 • La Pose, 1917 (?)
Oil on canvas, 65 x 54 cm

291 • My Room at the Beau-Rivage, 1917-1918
Oil on canvas, 73 x 61 cm
The Museum of Art, Philadelphia

292 • George Besson II, 1917-1918
Oil on panel, 15 x 10 cm
Musée des Beaux-Arts et d'Archéologie, Besançon

293 • Interior with Violin, 1917-1918
Oil on canvas, 116 x 89 cm
Statens Museum for Kunst, Copenhagen

294 • Nude in the Studio, 1917-1918
Oil on canvas, 41 x 33 cm

295 • Garden at Issy, 1917-1919
Oil on canvas, 130 x 89 cm
Private Collection

296 • Nude Standing, 1918
Oil on canvas, 41 x 27 cm

297 • Seated Nude with Back Turned, 1918
Oil on canvas, 62.2 x 47 cm
The Museum of Art, Philadelphia

298 • Nude in an Armchair, 1918
Oil on canvas, 46 x 38 cm
The Barnes Foundation, Merion

299 • Violinist at the Window, 1918
Oil on canvas, 150 x 98 cm
Musée national d'Art moderne, Paris

300 • The Window over the Sea, 1918
Oil on canvas, 73 x 60 cm
Hôtel Méditerranée Collection, Nice

301 • Interior with Black Notebook, 1918
Oil on canvas, 32.5 x 40 cm
Private Collection

302 • Large Landscape, Mont Alban, 1918
Oil on canvas, 73 x 90.8 cm
Private Collection

286 287 288 289

290 291 292

293 294

295 296 297

298 299

300 301 302

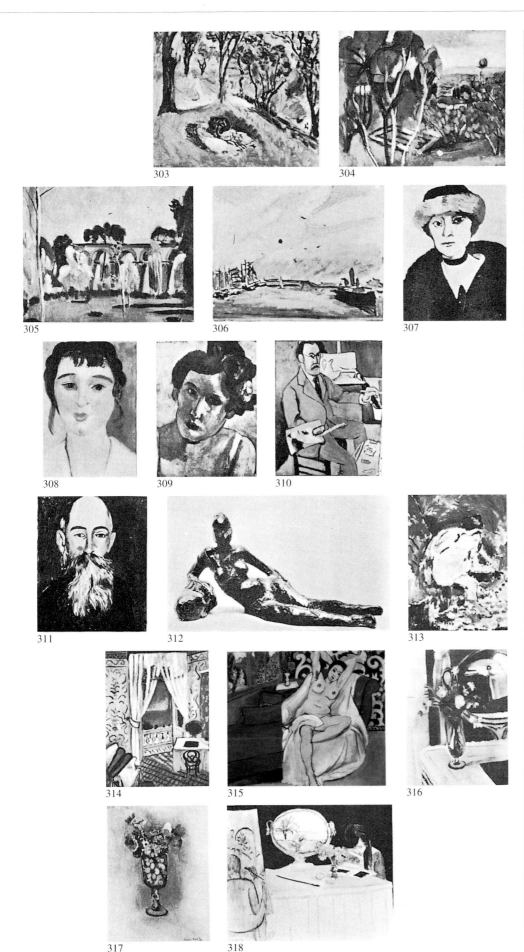

303

304

305

306

307

308

309

310

311

312

313

314

315

316

317

318

303 • Landscape around Nice, 1918
Oil on canvas, 38 x 46.5 cm

304 • Landscape of Montalban, 1918
Oil on canvas
Private Collection

**305 • The Aquaduct
at Maintenon, 1918**
Oil on canvas, 35 x 42 cm
The Museum of Art, Baltimore

**306 • The Ship with Yellow
Chimneys, 1918**
Oil on cardboard, 33 x 41 cm
Vismara Collection, Milan

**307 • Marguerite with
Leather Toga, 1918**
Oil on canvas
Private Collection

308 • Head of a Woman, 1918
Oil on canvas, 35.5 x 26.5 cm

309 • Head of a Woman, 1918
Oil on canvas
Reid Collection, London

310 • Self-Portrait, 1918
Oil on canvas, 65 x 54 cm
Musée Matisse, Le Cateau-Cambrésis

311 • The Antiquarian Demotte, 1918
Oil on panel, 55 x 46 cm
Musée des Beaux-Arts, Lyon

312 • Nude Lying on a Bolster, 1918
Bronze, 13 cm

**313 • Woman at the Fountain,
1918-1919**
Oil on canvas, 81 x 65 cm
Goulandris Collection, Lausanne

**314 • Interior with a Violin Case,
1918-1919**
Oil on canvas, 73 x 60 cm
The Museum of Modern Art, New York

**315 • Nude with Sheet on Red
Divan, 1918-1919**
Oil on canvas, 54 x 65 cm
Private Collection

**316 • Vase of Flowers on
a Dressing Table, 1919**
Oil on canvas, 65 x 50 cm

317 • Anemones in a Glass Jar, 1919
Oil on canvas, 61 x 46 cm
The Barnes Foundation, Merion

318 • The Painting Session, 1919
Oil on canvas, 74 x 93 cm
*National Gallery of Scotland,
Edinburgh*

319 • Female Figure Lying Down in the Open air, 1919
Oil on canvas, 31 x 41 cm
The Barnes Foundation, Merion

320 • Woman Seated in an Interior (The Striped Dress), 1919
Oil on canvas, 33 x 55 cm
The Barnes Foundation, Merion

321 • The Red Armchair, 1919
Oil on canvas, 35 x 56 cm
The Barnes Foundation, Merion

322 • Woman Seated, 1919
Oil on canvas, 46 x 66 cm
Rothschild Collection, London

323 • Interior : Window (Nice), 1919
Oil on canvas, 61 x 49 cm
Formerly Besson Collection, Paris

324 • The Blinds, 1919
Oil on canvas, 130 x 89 cm
The Barnes Foundation, Merion

325 • Tea in the Garden, 1919
Oil on canvas, 140.3 x 211.5 cm
County Museum of Art, Los Angeles

326 • White Feathers, 1919
Oil on canvas, 73 x 60.3 cm
The Institute of Arts, Minneapolis

327 • White Feathers, 1919
Oil on canvas, 74 x 60.5 cm
Konstmuseum, Göteborg

328 • The Plumed Hat, 1919
Oil on canvas, 47.7 x 38 cm
National Gallery of Art, Washington

329 • Antoinette, 1919
Oil on canvas, 66 x 50 cm

330 • The Green Shawl, 1919
Oil on canvas, 48.5 x 42.5 cm
The Art Institute, Chicago

331 • The Black Table (Woman with Oriental Dress), 1919
Oil on canvas, 100 x 81 cm
Private Collection

332 • Woman Seated, 1919
Oil on canvas, 56 x 39 cm
Mattioli Collection, Milan

333 • Nude with Spanish Rug, 1919
Oil on canvas, 65 x 54 cm
Private Collection

334 • Interior: Woman Seated, 1919
Oil on canvas, 65.7 x 46 cm
The Museum of Art, Philadelphia

319

320

321

322

323

324

325

326

327

328

329

330

331

332

333

334

335   336

337   338   339   340

341   342   343

344   345

346   347   348

349   350

335 • Woman Before the Dressing Table, 1919
Oil on canvas, 73 x 60 cm
The Barnes Foundation, Merion

336 • Girl and Folding Screen, 1919
Oil on canvas, 33 x 41 cm
The Barnes Foundation, Merion

337 • The 14th of July, 1919
Oil on canvas, 115 x 88 cm
Bernheim de Villers Collection, Monte-Carlo

338 • Plaster Figure, Bouquet of Flowers, 1919
Oil on canvas, 113 x 87 cm
Museu de Arte, São Paulo

339 • Chair with Peaches, 1919
Oil on canvas, 130 x 89 cm
Müller Collection, Soluthern

340 • The Painter and His Model: Studio Interior, 1919 (?)
Oil on canvas, 60 x 73 cm
Mr. and Mrs. Donald B. Marron Collection, New York

341 • Storm at Nice, 1919-1920
Oil on canvas, 60.5 x 73.5 cm
Musée Matisse, Nice

342 • Woman with a Green Parasol on a Balcony, 1919-1921
Oil on canvas, 66.5 x 47 cm
Private Collection

343 • The Prawns, 1920
Oil on canvas, 59 x 73 cm
Everhart Museum, Scranton (Pennsylvania)

344 • Pink Shrimp, 1920
Oil on canvas, 46 x 66 cm
Feigen Collection, New York

345 • Woman in a Flowered Hat, 1919-1920 (?)
Oil on canvas, 58.9 x 49.9 cm
Klapper Collection, New York

346 • The Bulgarian Blouse, 1920
Oil on canvas, 41 x 33 cm
Fitzwilliam Museum, Cambridge

347 • Odalisque, 1920
Oil on canvas, 56 x 66 cm
The Barnes Foundation, Merion

348 • The Meditation: After the Bath, 1920-1921
Oil on canvas, 73 x 54 cm
Private Collection

349 • The Green Dress, 1920
Oil on canvas, 41 x 34 cm
The Barnes Foundation, Merion

350 • Interior with Figure of Woman, 1920
Oil on canvas, 46 x 38 cm
The Barnes Foundation, Merion

WORKS

351 • Girl Near a Window, 1920
Oil on canvas, 63 x 48 cm
Private Collection

352 • Nude Standing Before a Window, 1920
Oil on canvas, 46 x 38 cm
The Barnes Foundation, Merion

353 • Interior at Nice (Mesdemoiselles Matisse and Daricarer or The Two Friends), 1920
Oil on canvas, 46.5 x 65.5 cm
Musée de l'Annonciade, Saint-Tropez

354 • Woman with Bunch of Anemones, 1920
Oil on canvas, 33.5 x 55.5 cm

355 • Woman Reading in the Open Air, 1920
Oil on canvas, 46 x 61 cm

356 • House in the Country, 1920
Oil on canvas, 33 x 41 cm
Private Collection

357 • Avenue between Olive Trees, 1920
Oil on canvas, 74 x 60 cm
Musée d'Art moderne de la Ville de Paris

358 • Cliff at Étretat, 1920
Oil on canvas, 43 x 63 cm
Musée d'Art Ohara, Kurashiki

359 • Marguerite on the Rocks, 1920
Oil on canvas, 37.7 x 45.7 cm
Private Collection

360 • Woman Standing, 1920 (?)
Oil (?), 65 x 47 cm

361 • Étretat : Fish in the Sand, 1920 (?)
53 x 65 cm

362 • Rocks, 1920-1921
Oil on canvas, 38 x 46 cm
The Museum of Art, Baltimore

363 • The Rock with the Hole, 1920-1921
Oil on canvas, 46 x 38 cm
The Museum of Art, Baltimore

364 • Boats on the Beach at Étretat, 1920-1921
Oil on canvas, 33 x 41 cm
The Barnes Foundation, Merion

365 • Fishing Nets at Étretat, 1920-1921
Oil on canvas, 32.5 x 41 cm
The Barnes Foundation, Merion

366 • The Sea (Étretat), 1920-1921
Oil on canvas, 40 x 44 cm
The Barnes Foundation, Merion

351

352

353

354

355

356

357

358

359

360

361

362

363

364

365

366

367

368

369

370

371

372

373

374

375

376

377

378

379

380

381

382

367 • Large Cliff: Fish, 1920 (1921?)
Oil on canvas, 93.1 x 73.7 cm
The Museum of Art, Baltimore

368 • Large Cliff: The Two Rays, 1920 (1921?)
Oil on canvas, 92.7 x 73.7 cm
Norton Gallery of Art, West Palm Beach, Florida

369 • Woman on Sofa, 1920-1922
Oil on canvas, 60 x 73.5 cm
Kunstmuseum, Basel

370 • At the Gorgues du Loup, 1920-1925
Oil on canvas, 50.2 x 61 cm
National Gallery of Art, Washington

371 • Open Window, Étretat, 1921
Oil on canvas, 46 x 38 cm
Bernheim-Jeune Collection, Paris

372 • Still Life with Lemon, 1921
Oil on canvas, 60 x 73 cm
Deutsch Collection, Greenwich (Connecticut)

373 • Girl at the Piano, 1921
Oil on canvas
Clarke Collection, New York

374 • Woman and Goldfish, 1921
Oil on canvas, 80.7 x 100 cm
The Art Institute, Chicago

375 • Nude Lying Down with Turban, 1921
Oil on canvas, 38 x 62 cm
Private Collection

376 • Nude with Turban, 1921
Oil on canvas, 92 x 73 cm

377 • Nude in a White Turban, 1921
Oil on canvas, 60 x 73 cm
Musée de l'Orangerie, Paris

378 • The Breakfast, 1921 (?)
Oil on canvas, 64 x 74 cm
The Museum of Art, Philadelphia

379 • Woman on a Pink Divan, 1921
Oil on canvas, 37.8 x 45.8 cm
The Art Institute, Chicago

380 • Two Women in an Interior, 1921
Oil on canvas, 92 x 73 cm
Musée de l'Orangerie, Paris

381 • Interior with Spanish, 1921
Oil on canvas, 74 x 60 cm
The Museum of Art, Baltimore

382 • Spanish Dancer, 1921
Oil on canvas, 53 x 95 cm
Musée du Louvre, Paris

WORKS

383 • The Boudoir, 1921
Oil on canvas, 73 x 60 cm
Musée de l'Orangerie, Paris

**384 • Interior at Nice: Young
Woman in a Green Dress Leaning
at the Window, 1921**
Oil on canvas, 65 x 55 cm
The Colin Collection, New York

385 • Girl Dressed in Blue, 1921
Oil on canvas, 61 x 50 cm
The Museum of Art, Baltimore

**386 • Girl Looking at Les Ponchettes
through the Window, 1921**
Oil on canvas, 33 x 54 cm
Private Collection

387 • Woman with Mandolin, 1921
Oil on canvas, 47 x 40 cm
Musée de l'Orangerie, Paris

**388 • Large Interior,
Nice, 1919-1921 (?)**
Oil on canvas, 132 x 89 cm
The Art Institute, Chicago

**389 • The Two Odalisques
(The Terrace), 1921**
Oil on canvas, 81.3 x 101.6 cm
Hester Diamond Collection, New York

390 • The Alhambra, 1921
Oil on canvas, 46 x 38 cm

391 • The Siesta in the Open Air, 1921
Oil on canvas, 38 x 47 cm
The Barnes Foundation, Merion

392 • The Moorish Screen, 1921-1922
Oil on canvas, 90.8 x 74.3 cm
The Museum of Art, Philadelphia

393 • The Domino Players, 1921-1922
Oil on canvas, 59 x 72 cm
The Barnes Foundation, Merion

**394 • Interior in Nice: The Siesta,
1921-1922**
Oil on canvas, 66 x 54.5 cm
Musée national d'Art moderne, Paris

**395 • Interior at Nice : Woman
at the Window, 1921-1922**
Oil on canvas, 65 x 52 cm
The Barnes Foundation, Merion

**396 • Odalisque (The White Slave),
1921-1922**
Oil on canvas, 82 x 54 cm
Musée de l'Orangerie, Paris

**397 • Woman at the Window,
1921-1922**
Oil on canvas, 50.5 x 61 cm
Musée de l'Annonciade, Saint-Tropez

383

384

385

386

387

388

389

390

391

392

393

394

395

396

397

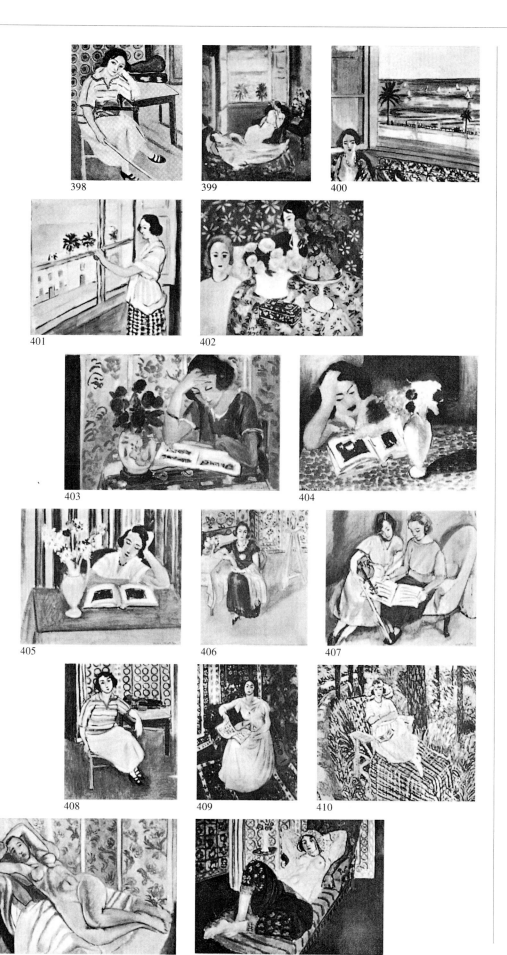

398

399

400

401

402

403

404

405

406

407

408

409

410

411

412

398 • The Violiniste Repose, 1921-1923
Oil on canvas, 55 x 40 cm
Musée de l'Orangerie, Paris

399 • Confidences, 1922
Oil on canvas, 55 x 46 cm
The Barnes Foundation, Merion

400 • Woman Before the Window, Nice, 1922
Oil on canvas, 72 x 92 cm
The Museum of Fine Arts, Montreal

401 • Girl Before the Window, Afternoon, 1922
Oil on canvas, 50 x 61 cm
The Museum of Art, Baltimore

402 • The Chinese Box, 1922
Oil on canvas, 60 x 73 cm

403 • The Chinese Chair, 1922
Oil on canvas, 33.5 x 56 cm
Feigen Collection, Chicago

404 • Woman Reading, 1922
Oil on canvas, 24 x 33 cm
Private Collection

405 • Girl Reading, 1922
Oil on canvas, 38 x 46 cm
The Museum of Art, Baltimore

406 • The Taffeta Dress, 1922
Oil on canvas, 46 x 38 cm
The Museum of Art, Baltimore

407 • The Musicians, 1922
Oil on canvas, 54 x 65 cm
The Museum of Art, Baltimore

408 • Woman with Violin, 1922
Oil on canvas, 73 x 60 cm
The Museum of Art, Baltimore

409 • Woman with Guitar, 1922
Oil on canvas, 66 x 51 cm

410 • Woman Seated in the Garden, 1922
Oil on canvas

411 • Nude Lying Down, 1922
Oil on canvas, 59 x 91 cm
The Barnes Foundation, Merion

412 • Odalisque with Red Trousers, 1922
Oil on canvas, 67 x 84 cm
Musée national d'Art moderne, Paris

WORKS

413 • Arabian Woman, 1922
Oil on canvas, 46 x 38 cm
The Barnes Foundation, Merion

414 • Arabian Woman, 1922
Oil on canvas, 35.6 x 24.4 cm
National Gallery of Art, Washington

415 • Odalisque with Tambourin, 1922
Oil on canvas, 55 x 38 cm
The Museum of Art, Baltimore

**416 • Nude on a
Red Background, 1922**
Oil on canvas

417 • Festival of Flowers, 1922
Oil on canvas, 65 x 92 cm
The Museum of Art, Baltimore

**418 • Festival of Flowers,
1921 (1922 ?)**
Oil on canvas, 72.5 x 99 cm
Private Collection

**419 • The Painter in the Olive
Grove, 1922**
Oil on canvas, 61 x 71 cm
The Museum of Art, Baltimore

420 • Repose Beneath the Trees, 1922
Oil on canvas, 38 x 46 cm
The Museum of Art, Baltimore

**421 • Conversation Under
the Olive Trees, 1921-1922 (?)**
Oil on canvas, 100 x 81 cm
*Thyssen-Bornemisza Collection,
Lugano*

422 • The «Dorado», 1922
Oil on canvas, 60 x 73 cm
Formerly Granoff Collection, Paris

423 • Anemones and Chinese Jar, 1922
Oil on canvas, 61 x 92 cm
The Museum of Art, Baltimore

**424 • Apples on a Pink
Tablecloth, 1922**
Oil on canvas, 60.4 x 73 cm
National Gallery of Art, Washington

425 • Étretat, 1922-1923
Oil on canvas, 46 x 38 cm
Bernheim-Jeune Collection, Paris

**426 • Woman Before
the Window, 1923**
Oil on canvas, 46 x 66 cm

**427 • Two Women Before
the Window, 1923**
Oil on canvas, 61 x 49 cm
The Barnes Foundation, Merion

413

414

415

416

417

418

419

420

421

422

423

424

425

426

427

428

429

430

431

432

433

434

435

436

437

438

439

440

441

442

428 • Young Woman Painter, 1923
Oil on canvas
Newton Collection, New York

**429 • Painter Working Near
a Stream, 1923**
Oil on canvas, 59 x 72 cm
Private Collection

430 • The Repose, 1923
Oil on canvas, 26 x 47 cm
The Barnes Foundation, Merion

431 • Woman Seated on a Sofa, 1923
Oil on canvas, 73 x 60 cm
The Museum of Art, Philadelphia

432 • The Piano Lesson, 1923
Oil on canvas, 65 x 81 cm
Middleton Collection, Dundee

**433 • The Spaniard, Harmony
in White, 1923**
Oil on canvas, 59 x 49 cm
Private Collection

**434 • The Spaniard, Harmony
in Blue, 1923**
Oil on canvas
Fondation Robert Lehman, New York

435 • Odalisque, 1923
Oil on canvas, 61 x 74 cm
Stedelijk Museum, Amsterdam

**436 • The Odalisque Before
the Mirror, 1923**
Oil on canvas, 81 x 55 cm
The Museum of Art, Baltimore

437 • Odalisque with Open Arms, 1923
Oil on canvas, 65 x 50 cm
National Gallery of Art, Washington

438 • The Hindu Pose, 1923
Oil on canvas, 83 x 60 cm
Private Collection

439 • Anemones and Chinese Jar, 1923
Oil on canvas, 75 x 60 cm
Private Collection

**440 • Still Life: Bouquet of Dahlias
and White Book, 1923**
Oil on canvas, 50.2 x 61 cm
The Museum of Art, Baltimore

441 • Reader with Peaches, 1923
Oil on canvas, 12.7 x 17.2 cm
Stephen Hahn Collection, New York

442 • Nude Lying Down, 1923-1924
Oil on canvas, 39 x 61 cm
Musée de l'Orangerie, Paris

WORKS

443 • Large Seated Nude, 1924-1929
Bronze, 79.4 x 77.5 x 34.9 cm
The Museum of Modern Art, New York

**444 • Pianist and
Checker Players, 1924**
Oil on canvas, 73 x 92 cm
National Gallery of Art, Washington

445 • Hebrew Stories, 1924
Oil on canvas, 82 x 101 cm
The Museum of Art, Philadelphia

446 • Pascal's Thoughts, 1924
Oil on canvas, 50 x 65 cm
Private Collection

**447 • Anemones in an
Earthenware Vase, 1924**
Oil on canvas, 74 x 92 cm
Kunstmuseum, Bern

448 • Vase in an Interior, 1924
Oil on canvas
Museum of Fine Arts, Boston

449 • Moroccan Plate, 1924
Oil on canvas, 49 x 61 cm
Private Collection

**450 • Interior with a
Phonograph, 1924**
Oil on canvas, 100.5 x 81 cm
Private Collection

**451 • Interior: Flowers
and Parakeets, 1924**
Oil on canvas, 116.9 x 72.7 cm
The Museum of Art, Baltimore

**452 • Portrait of the Baronne
Gourgaud, 1924**
Oil on canvas, 81 x 65 cm
Musée national d'Art moderne, Paris

453 • The Pink Blouse, 1924
Oil on canvas, 56 x 46.5 cm
The Museum of Modern Art, New York

454 • Woman with Kimono, 1924
Oil on canvas, 46 x 38 cm

455 • The Afternoon Session, 1924
Oil on canvas

456 • Odalisque with Magnolias, 1924
Oil on canvas, 65 x 81 cm
Private Collection

**457 • Odalisque on a Striped
Armchair, c. 1924**
Oil on canvas, 65 x 46 cm
The Museum of Art, Baltimore

443

444

445

446

447

448

449

450

451

452

453

454

455

456

457

458

459

460

461

462

463

464

465

466

467

468

469

470

471

472

WORKS

**473 • Odalisque with
a Tambourine, 1926**
Oil on canvas, 74.3 x 55.7 cm
The Museum of Modern Art, New York

474 • Dancer with Tambourine, 1926
Oil on canvas, 92 x 65 cm
Private Collection

**475 • The Cap d'Antibes Road.
The Great Tree, 1926**
Oil on canvas, 50 x 61 cm
Private Collection

476 • Renoir's Garden, 1926-1927
Oil on panel, 37 x 45 cm
*Musée national des Beaux-Arts,
Algiers*

477 • Pineapple on Basket, 1926-1928
Oil on canvas, 47 x 38 cm

**478 • Nude Seated with
Open Arms, 1927**
Oil on canvas, 35 x 24 cm
Lefebvre-Foinet Collection, Paris

479 • Woman with a Veil, 1927
Oil on canvas, 61.5 x 50.2 cm
The Museum of Modern Art, New York

480 • Classic Ballerina, 1927
Oil on canvas, 81 x 61 cm
The Museum of Art, Baltimore

**481 • Ballerina Standing;
Harmony in Gray, 1927**
Oil on canvas, 56 x 38 cm
Private Collection

482 • Lemons on a Tin Plate, 1927
Oil on canvas, 43 x 66 cm
H. Ault Collection, New Canaan

**483 • Odalisque with Gray
Trousers, 1927**
Oil on canvas, 54 x 65 cm
Musée de l'Orangerie, Paris

484 • Odalisque with Red Chest, 1927
Oil on canvas, 50 x 65 cm
Musée Matisse, Nice

485 • Nude Lying on Her Back, 1927
Oil on canvas, 66 x 92 cm
Private Collection

486 • Reclining Nude II, 1927
Bronze, 28 cm
Private Collection

487 • Henriette II, 1927
Bronze, 36 cm
Private Collection

473

474

475

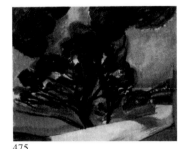
476

477

478

479

480

481

482

483

484

485

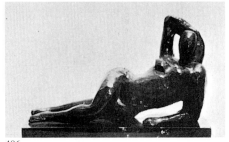
486

487

488

489

490

491

492

493

494

495

496

497

498

499

500

501

502

488 • Odalisque with Turkish Armchair, 1928
Oil on canvas, 60 x 73 cm
Musée d'Art moderne de la Ville de Paris

489 • Odalisque Seated, 1928
Oil on canvas, 55 x 37 cm
The Museum of Art, Baltimore

490 • Game of Draughts, 1928
Oil on canvas, 56 x 73 cm
The Colin Collection, New York

491 • Still Life on a Green Sideboard, 1928
Oil on canvas, 81.5 x 100 cm
Musée national d'Art moderne, Paris

492 • Gladioli, 1928
Oil on canvas, 155 x 100 cm
Chrysler Art Museum, Provincetown

493 • Harmony in Yellow, 1928
Oil on canvas, 88 x 88 cm
Sandblom Collection, Lund

494 • Nude in the Studio, 1928
Oil on canvas, 60 x 82 cm

495 • Large Gray Nude, 1929
Oil on canvas, 102 x 81 cm
Private Collection

496 • Nude Before the Window, 1929
Oil on canvas, 66 x 53 cm
Horowitz Collection, New York

497 • Henriette III, 1929
Bronze, 40 cm
Private Collection

498 • Reclining Nude III, 1929
Bronze, 18.7 x 46.5 x 15.1 cm
Private Collection

499 • The Moor, 1929
Oil on canvas, 92 x 65 cm
Private Collection

500 • Woman with a Madras Hat, 1929-1930
Oil on canvas, 180 x 152 cm
Private Collection

501 • The Yellow Dress, 1929-1931
Oil on canvas, 99.7 x 80.7 cm
The Museum of Art, Baltimore

502 • The Back IV, 1930
Bronze, 190 x 112 cm
Musée national d'Art moderne, Paris

WORKS

503 • Tiari, 1930
Bronze, 20 x 14 x 13 cm
Private Collection

504 • Asia, 1930
Bronze, 33 cm
Private Collection

505 • Venus in the Shell II, 1932
Bronze, 34 cm
Private Collection

506 • Dance (first version), 1931-1932-1933
Oil on panel,
340 x 387. 355 x 498. 333 x 391 cm
Musée d'Art moderne de la Ville de Paris

507 • Dance, 1932-1933
Oil on canvas, 339.7 x 441.3, 355.9 x 503.2, 338.8 x 439.4 cm
The Barnes Foundation, Merion

508 • Interior with a Dog (The Magnolia Branch), 1934
Oil on canvas, 155 x 167 cm
The Museum of Art, Baltimore

509 • The Blue Eyes, 1935
Oil on canvas, 38.1 x 45.7 cm
The Museum of Art, Baltimore

510 • The Dream, 1935
Oil on canvas, 81 x 65 cm
Musée national d'Art moderne, Paris

511 • Pink Nude, 1935
Oil on canvas, 66 x 92 cm
The Museum of Art, Baltimore

512 • Window at Tahiti, 1935
Oil on canvas, 225 x 172 cm
Musée Matisse, Nice

513 • Pink Seated Nude, 1935-1936
Oil on canvas, 92 x 73 cm
Private Collection

514 • Nymph in the Forest, 1935-1943
Oil on canvas, 242 x 195 cm
Musée Matisse, Nice

515 • Painter and Model, 1936
Oil on canvas, 60 x 81 cm
Wallach Collection, New York

516 • Woman on a Red Chair, 1936
Oil on canvas, 34 x 23 cm
The Museum of Art, Baltimore

517 • Nude with Empire Necklace, 1936
Oil on canvas

 503
 504
 505
 506
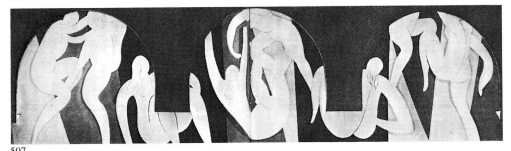 507
 508
 509
 510
 511
 512
 513
 514
 515
 516

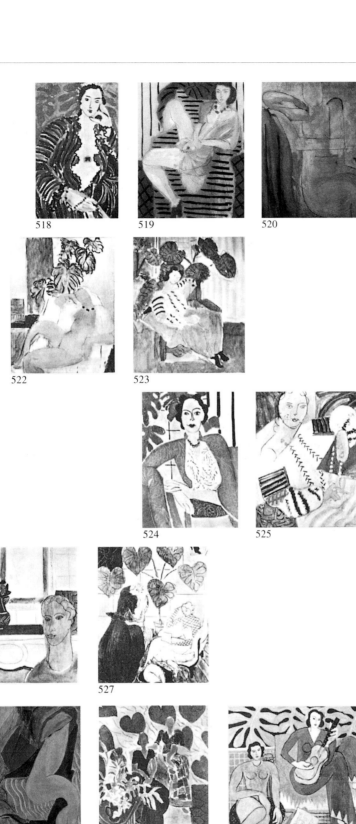

518   519   520

521   522   523

524   525

526   527

528   529   530

531   532

518 • Hélène, 1936
Oil on canvas, 55 x 30 cm

519 • Woman in an Armchair or White and Yellow Background, 1936
Oil on canvas, 46 x 38 cm
Private Collection

520 • Seated Pink Nude, 1935-1936 (?)
Oil on canvas, 46 x 38 cm
Private Collection

521 • Tahiti II, 1936
Gouache on canvas, 238 x 185 cm
Musée Matisse, Le Cateau-Cambrésis

522 • Nude in an Armchair and Plant, 1936-1937
Oil on canvas, 72.5 x 60.5 cm
Musée Matisse, Nice

523 • Girl with a Green and Yellow Dress, 1937
Oil on canvas, 46 x 38 cm

524 • The Amber Necklace, 1937
Oil on canvas, 65 x 50 cm
Rosenberg Collection, New York

525 • The Romanian Blouse, 1937
Oil on canvas, 73 x 60 cm
Art Museum, Cincinnati

526 • The Ochre Head, 1937
Oil on canvas, 72.7 x 54 cm
Private Collection

527 • The Conservatory, 1937-1938
Oil on canvas, 71.8 x 59.7 cm
Private Collection

528 • The Arm, 1938
Oil on canvas, 46 x 38 cm
Private Collection

529 • Two Feminine Figures on a Leafy Background, 1938
Oil on canvas, 55 x 46 cm
Rosenberg Collection, New York

530 • Music, 1939
Oil on canvas, 115.1 x 115.1 cm
Albright-Knox Art Gallery, Buffalo

531 • Woman in Yellow and Blue with Guitar, 1939
Oil on canvas, 65 x 54 cm
Private Collection

532 • Daisies, 1939
Oil on canvas, 98 x 71.8 cm
The Art Institute, Chicago

WORKS

533 • Interior at Ciboure, 1940
Oil on canvas, 73 x 60 cm
Musée Toulouse-Lautrec, Albi

**534 • Woman in a Yellow
Armchair, 1940**
Oil on canvas, 54 x 64 cm
*Maugham Collection,
Saint-Jean-Cap-Ferrat*

535 • The Romanian Blouse, 1940
Oil on canvas, 92 x 73 cm
Musée national d'Art moderne, Paris

536 • The Dream, 1940
Oil on canvas, 81 x 65 cm
Private Collection

537 • Persian Dress, 1940
Oil on canvas, 73 x 60 cm

538 • Still Life with Oysters, 1940
Oil on canvas, 65.5 x 81.5 cm
Kunstmuseum, Basel

539 • Pineapple and Anemones, 1940
Oil on canvas, 73.7 x 91.4 cm
Private Collection

**540 • Interior with an
Etruscan Vase, 1940**
Oil on canvas, 73.6 x 108 cm
The Museum of Art, Cleveland

541 • Still Life with Magnolia, 1941
Oil on canvas, 74 x 101 cm
Musée national d'Art moderne, Paris

**542 • Dancer and Rocaille Armchair
on a Black Background, 1942**
Oil on canvas, 50.8 x 64.8 cm
Private Collection

543 • The Idol, 1942
Oil on canvas, 71 x 91 cm
Lasker Collection, New York

544 • The Black Door, 1942
Oil on canvas, 61 x 38 cm
*Contemporary Art Establishment,
Zurich*

**545 • Woman with Pearls
Necklace, 1942**
Oil on canvas, 62 x 50 cm
Private Collection

**546 • Lemons on a Rose
Background, 1943**
Oil on canvas, 66 x 50 cm
Lasker Collection, New York

547 • Lemons and Hydrangea, 1943
Oil on canvas, 54 x 81 cm
Rosengart Collection, Lucerne

533

534

535

536

537

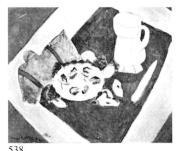
538

539

540

541

542

543

544

545

546

547

548

549

550

551

552

553

554

555

556

557

558

559

560

561

562

548 • The Lute, 1943
Oil on canvas, 59.4 x 79.5 cm
Private Collection

549 • Michaela, 1943
Oil on canvas, 60 x 72 cm
Private Collection

**550 • Icarus
(Plate VIII from Jazz), 1943**
Gouache on paper, cut and pasted, on
white paper, 43.4 x 34.1 cm
Musée national d'Art moderne, Paris

551 • The Painting Session, 1943
Oil on canvas, 54 x 73 cm
Private Collection

**552 • Lemons and Mimosa on
a Black Background, 1944**
Oil on canvas, 54 x 73 cm

**553 • Girl with Tulips
and Anemones, 1944**
Oil on canvas, 84 x 97 cm
Academy of Arts, Honolulu

554 • Asia, 1946
Oil on canvas, 116 x 81 cm
*Parnis Livingston Collection,
New York*

**555 • Interior in Yellow
and Blue, 1946**
Oil on canvas, 116 x 81 cm
Musée national d'Art moderne, Paris

**556 • Young Woman in White,
Red Background, 1946**
Oil on canvas, 92 x 73 cm
Musée national d'Art moderne, Paris

557 • The Rocaille Armchair, 1946
Oil on canvas, 92 x 73 cm
Musée Matisse, Nice

558 • Red Interior, 1947
Oil on canvas, 116 x 89 cm
*Kunstsammlung Nordrhein-Westfalen,
Düsseldorf*

**559 • Still Life with
Pomegranate, 1947**
Oil on canvas, 80.5 x 60 cm
Musée Matisse, Nice

**560 • The Young English
Woman, 1947**
Oil on canvas, 55 x 33 cm
Private Collection

**561 • Inhabited Silence
of Houses, 1947**
Oil on canvas, 61 x 50 cm
Private Collection

562 • Black Boxer, 1947
Gouache on paper, cut and pasted,
on white paper
Musée national d'Art moderne, Paris

563 • Crucifix, 1947-1951
Bronze
*Chapelle du Rosaire des
Dominicaines, Vence (Nice)*

**564 • Peach Branch on Ochre
Background, 1948**
Oil on canvas, 116 x 89 cm
Private Collection

565 • Large Interior in Red, 1948
Oil on canvas, 146 x 97 cm
Musée national d'Art moderne, Paris

**566 • Interior with an Egyptian
Curtain, 1948**
Oil on canvas, 116.2 x 89.2 cm
The Phillips Collection, Washington

567 • Pineapple, 1948
Oil on canvas, 116 x 89 cm
*Alex Hillman Family Foundation,
New York*

568 • The Black Fern, 1948
Oil on canvas, 116 x 89 cm
Bayeler Collection, Basel

569 • Nude Standing (Katia), 1950
Bronze, 45 cm
Private Collection

570 • Creole Dancer, 1950
Gouache on paper, cut and pasted,
on white paper, 205 x 120 cm
Musée Matisse, Nice

571 • Zulma, 1950
Gouache on paper, cut and pasted,
on white paper, 238 x 130 cm
*Statens Museum for Kunst,
Copenhagen*

572 • The Beasts of the Sea, 1950
Gouache on paper, cut and pasted,
on white paper, 295.5 x 154 cm
National Gallery of Art, Washington

**573 • Study for the Tabernacle
of the Rosaire Chapel, 1950**
Gouache on paper, cut and pasted,
on white paper
Private Collection

574 • Christmas Eve, 1951-1952
Maquette for a stained-glass window:
gouache on paper, cut and pasted,
322.6 x 135.9 cm
The Museum of Modern Art, New York

**575 • Composition, Blue
Background, 1951**
Gouache on paper, cut and pasted,
on white paper, 80 x 50 cm
Private Collection

576 • The Sadness of the King, 1952
Gouache on paper, cut and pasted,
on white paper, 292 x 386 cm
Musée national d'Art moderne, Paris

577 • Acrobats, 1952
Gouache on paper, cut and pasted, and
charcoal on white paper, 213 x 209.5 cm
Private Collection

563

564

565

566

567

568

569

570

571

572

573

574

575

576

577

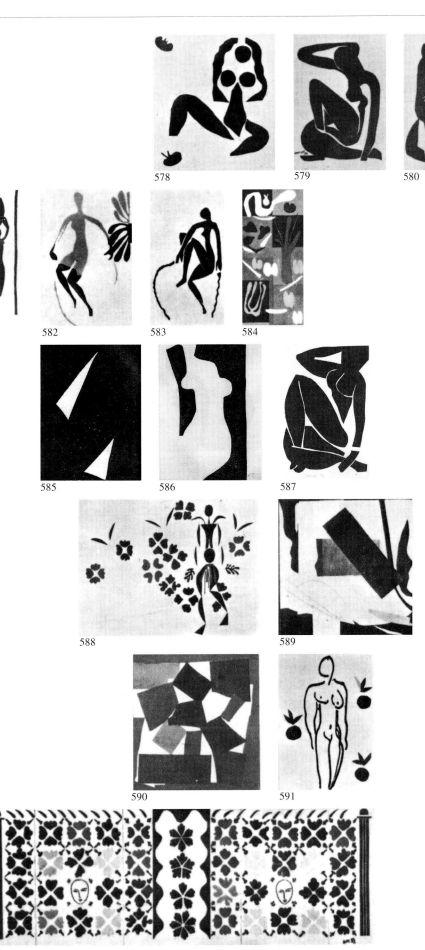

578

579

580

581

582

583

584

585

586

587

588

589

590

591

592

578 • The Frog, 1952
Gouache on paper, cut and pasted,
on white paper, 141 x 134 cm
Preminger Collection, New York

579 • Blue Nude I, 1952
Gouache on paper, cut and pasted,
on white paper, 106 x 78 cm
Galerie Bayeler Collection, Basel

580 • The Flowing Hair, 1952
Gouache on paper, cut and pasted,
on white paper, 108 x 80 cm
Private Collection

**581 • Woman with Jar
and Pomegranates, 1952**
Gouache on paper, cut and pasted,
on white paper, 242 x 96 cm
Private Collection

582 • Blue Nude, 1952
Stenciled Gouache, 260 x 168 cm
Private Collection

583 • Girl Skipping, 1952
Gouache on paper, cut and pasted,
on white paper, 145 x 98 cm
Private Collection

584 • Vegetables, 1951-1952 (?)
Gouache on paper, cut and pasted,
on white paper, 175 x 81 cm
Private Collection

585 • The Sails, 1952
Gouache on paper, cut and pasted,
on white paper, 72 x 60 cm
Private Collection

586 • Vénus, 1952
Gouache on paper, cut and pasted,
on white paper, 101.2 x 76.5 cm
National Gallery of Art, Washington

587 • Blue Nude III, 1952
Gouache on paper cutout,
112 x 73.5 cm
Musée national d'Art moderne, Paris

588 • The Negress, 1952-1953
Stenciled Gouache, 453.9 x 623.6 cm
National Gallery of Art, Washington

589 • Memory of Oceania, 1952-1953
Gouache on paper, cut and pasted,
and charcoal on white paper,
284.4 x 286.4 cm
The Museum of Modern Art, New York

590 • The Snail, 1952-1953
Gouache on paper, cut and pasted,
on white paper, 286 x 288 cm
The Tate Gallery, London

591 • Nude, 1952-1953
Gouache on paper, cut and pasted, and
ink on white paper, 154.2 x 107.1 cm
Musée national d'Art moderne, Paris

**592 • Large Decoration
with Masks, 1953**
Gouache on paper, cut and pasted,
and brush and ink on white paper,
353.6 x 996.4 cm
National Gallery of Art, Washington

Bibliography

HENRI MATISSE:

Matisse on Art, D. Fourcade, ed., Paris, 1973

Bonnard/Matisse : Letters between Friends, 1925-1946, trans. R. Howard, New York, 1992

A. BARR, *Matisse : his Art and his Public*, catalogue of the Exhibition, The Museum of Modern Art, New York, 1951

C. BOCK, *Henri Matisse and Neo-Impressionism 1898-1908*, Ann Arbor (Mich.), 1981

J. ELDERFIELD, *Henri Matisse : A Retrospective*, catalogue of the Exhibition, The Museum of Modern Art, New York, 1992

A. ELSEN, *The Sculpture of Henri Matisse*, New York, 1972

J. FLAM, *Matisse on Art*, New York, 1973

J. FLAM, *Matisse, the Man and his Art 1869-1918*, Ithaca-London, 1986

X. GIRARD, S. KUTHY, *Henri Matisse, 1869-1954: Skulpturen und Druckgraphik / Sculptures et gravures*, catalogue of the Exhibition, Kunstmuseum, Bern, 1990

L. GOWING, *Matisse*, New York-Toronto, 1979

J. GUICHARD-MEILI, *L'art de Matisse*, Paris, 1993

E.G. GÜSE, ed., *Henri Matisse, Zeichnungen und Skulpturen*, Munich, 1991

Henri Matisse, catalogue of the Exhibition, Centre Georges Pompidou, Paris, 1993

Matisse in Morocco : The Paintings and Drawings 1912-1913, National Gallery of Art, Washington, 1990

I. MONOD-FONTAINE, *The Sculpture of Henri Matisse*, London, 1984

P. SCHNEIDER, *Matisse*, New York, 1984

P. SCHNEIDER, *Tout l'œuvre peint de Henri Matisse 1904-1928*, 2nd ed, Paris, 1992

Picture Credits